HOW I

SPENT MY WAY OUT OF DEBT

HOW I SPENT MY WAY OUT OF DEBT

A REAL ESTATE INVESTOR'S JOURNEY FROM RUINS TO RICHES

ROBERT KRANENDONK

BURMAN BOOKS
MEDIA CORP.

BURMAN BOOKS
MEDIA
MEDIA CORP.

Published 2024 by Gildan Media LLC, aka G&D Media
by arrangement with Burman Books Media Corp.
www.GandDmedia.com

Edited by Lara Petersen
Cover Photo by Jilly Maciver
Book Design by Clarissa D'Costa

Library of Congress Cataloging-in-Publication Data is available upon
request

ISBN: 978-1-7225-9902-7

10   9   8   7   6   5   4   3   2   1

CONTENTS

CHAPTER 1

NO FEAR!

Success begins with a mindset. Some people are born with it. Others learn to apply it.

I was born with an entrepreneurial spirit and an innate sense of how to make money.

Two occasions stick out in my mind. At age seven, my friend and I decided to put on a variety show. We designed our five-cent tickets to our show and went door to door selling them to our neighbors. The moms all thought it was a great initiative and gladly coughed up the five cents. Before we knew it, a massive crowd had gathered on our lawn to see our production. We stood behind the fence, held up puppets, and improvised a show that the kids loved. We had a great time and, together, made the most money we had ever seen in our young lives.

Then, a year later, my mom sent me off on a boys' summer camp for the first time. I was somewhat trepidatious. I wasn't too sure about this. To leave home for two whole weeks!? How could I possibly survive!? I pleaded, "Don't make me go!"

Mom reassured me. She told me about all the activities I would learn and participate in, and said it would be an amazing experience. She then moved to the bribing stage and explained that the camp has a tuck shop.

"A tuck shop?" I asked. "What is that?" A tuck shop is like a small variety store where campers buy candy, chocolate, chips, ice cream, etc. As well as being an income stream for the summer camp, a tuck shop provides campers with a sense of comfort.

Intrigued, I said "Oh . . . okay . . ."

Mom said, "I am going to put twenty dollars into your tuck account. Whenever you want a treat, you can buy something, and whatever you don't spend, you can keep."

I can keep!? Really?

I thought, wow! This is great! My first taste of freedom and independence, and an opportunity to keep some pocket change. Okay . . . I guess I will go to summer camp and see how it goes.

Mom left me at the drop-off spot in Toronto where all the campers boarded a bus. Ahead of us was a two-hour drive north to the Muskokas. I don't remember much about that ride; however, I do remember stepping off the bus feeling somewhat anxious about how the next couple of weeks would unfold.

At the beginning of the two weeks, I did not want to be there. When the two weeks were over, I did not want to leave. I ended up having an amazing time!

The camp directors instructed us to go to the tuck shop and withdraw what cash we had left in our accounts. I watched kid after kid file into the store, withdraw their leftover money, and stuff it into their pockets.

Growing up Dutch, I learned to be very frugal with my money. I hadn't spent much of the twenty dollars my mom deposited into my tuck account. I looked around at all those kids with money in their pockets. I looked around the tuck shop and eyed all kinds of candy, chips, Cheezies, liquorice, etc.

I stepped up to the cashier and withdrew my leftover funds... I held the fistful of dollar bills and looked up to survey the wonder of junk food before me. I walked around the shop and grabbed everything I could hold in my hands and spent every penny.

I made my way to the bus, boarded, took my seat, and stared out the window as the camp disappeared into the distance.

The bus ride was quiet for what seemed like an eternity. It seemed as if the camp was a positive experience for all and had left the kids in quiet contemplation. They began to stir about a half hour into the ride back to Toronto. The hyperactivity that you would expect from a bus full of eight- to ten-year-old boys unfolded.

I reached for the bag of treats at my feet and pulled it up to my seat.

Suddenly, the pandemonium halted. Boys were eyeing up my stash . . . "Can I have some?" One boy asked. "Yeah," said another, "I am starving!"

I looked up and said, "Sure! You got any tuck money left?"

The boys reached into their pockets and grabbed their dollar bills. "Yes!" many of them exclaimed.

"Okay," I calmly said. "What is it worth for you?"

The boys began outbidding each other to get their hands on one of the many treats I had invested in. Piece by piece, I exchanged my goods for wealth. They were happy and I was ecstatic! I was hungry, but I had no food left. I looked down and smiled at the wad of cash in my hand. I stuffed it into my pocket, relaxed in my seat, and stared out the window. I was pleased with the return on my investment.

The bus pulled up to the pick-up point in Toronto. The kids got off the bus and were greeted by their parents who asked how they liked the camp. I heard parents asking if their kids had any leftover tuck money. They all shook their heads and the parent said, "That's okay. I'm glad you had fun."

I turned around to see my mom standing behind me. I hugged her tightly and explained that I had the best time ever. Mom was so happy. She then asked me, "How much have you got leftover from your tuck account?" She was smiling, expecting me to say the same as all the other kids. I stuffed my hand into my pocket and pulled out the wad of my newfound wealth. Her eyes lit up and her jaw hit the floor. She said, "Didn't you buy anything from the tuck shop over the last two weeks?"

"Yes," I replied.

"Then how do you have so much money leftover?"

"Easy," I replied. "Today, I spent what I had left on junk food and sold it all on the bus."

"Wow!" My mom was in shock. "How much have you got there?"

I took a minute to count. "Twenty-two dollars," I proclaimed with beaming pride and the biggest smile on my face.

Mom couldn't believe it. Her timid little eight-year-old boy started off with twenty dollars and returned home with twenty-two dollars.

At that moment, I think Mom knew I was destined to be successful in life on my own terms.

KEY READER TAKEAWAYS

So, why do I bother opening my book with a story like this? What is the takeaway from this experience that makes real estate investing relevant to you?

There are several relevant and teachable moments, actually.

1. Fear of the unknown can be very difficult to overcome if you don't jump right in.

2. When you look back after exposing yourself to the situation, you can see that there was nothing to fear. You are resilient. You adapt to new surroundings, thrive, and enjoy the experience. Be open and adaptable.

3. Look for opportunities where others may not have. I took a risk by spending all my money on treats. I calculated the risk and thought it was worth the investment. My idea paid off and, to this day, my parents still laugh about my first successful investment. Be creative and think outside of the box.

People who come to me wanting to know how to get started in real estate investing have the same fear I had heading to summer camp for the first time. Fear of the unknown holds them back, even after seeing others succeed, such as myself. To be successful at real estate investing, you must force yourself to look past your fear. You must learn to see the opportunity, weigh the costs and benefits, and then take a leap of faith.

You don't have to be born with this mindset. Some people can learn to adopt the attitude.

You can do this!

Getting started in real estate investing starts with a mindset and hard work. The next chapter discusses how I carried my mindset as a child. I set a goal for myself at a young age and stuck with it.

CHAPTER 2
HARD WORK

My early experience of making money as a child gave me a taste for wanting to make more. But how? What could I do to earn more money?

The answer was simple. Whatever it takes!

If you want to get ahead in life, it starts with hard work, hustle, and discipline.

A couple of years after making my business investment at summer camp, I had it in my head that I needed to find ways to earn money.

At age eleven, I remember asking Mom if my older brother, my friend, and I could earn money somehow. She suggested that we go down to the Farmer's Pool, which was a gathering of people looking to make daily cash by picking fruit for local farmers.

We were selected to go in a van with a bunch of strangers (mostly adults). We were picking cherries and were paid according to how many quarts we filled. I was very excited by this prospect. I diligently picked as quickly as I could. My brother was less keen on filling his quarts and more interested in how many cherries he could eat. Seeing this, I paused for a moment, shoved a few in my mouth, and then kept filling my quarts.

I don't remember how much money I made, only that I was amazed by how I could give up my time and earn good money in one day. We did this several times throughout the summer and I loved the sweet taste of earning money. That summer, I opened my first bank account and deposited all my earnings.

That winter, my mom decided to travel to Nigeria to visit a neighborhood friend who had moved there with her family. She was gone for a month, so her four children were billeted to stay with other friends. My dad was home, but he was busy with work and the committees he was involved with.

The family that took me in owned a greenhouse and nursery business. After staying with them for several days, I asked if I could work for them in the summer. The husband hummed and hawed, and then asked how old I was. I said I would be twelve this summer. He nodded and continued thinking. It seemed like an eternity of silence passed. I just kept staring at him with my big brown eyes.

Finally, he nodded and said, "Okay, when you're done school in June, come to the nursery and we will give you a shot."

I was so incredibly excited. Wow! My first summer job.

When Mom returned from Nigeria, I told her my exciting news. Once again, she was impressed by my tenacity and determination. She thought it was fantastic.

When summer arrived, Mom dropped me and my brother off to work at the nursery.

I took my job very seriously. It was to scratch rosebushes. This meant I had to get on my hands and knees in a field of roses and crawl along, pulling the dirt away from the base of the plants. This was to prepare them for the process of crossbreeding to create new varieties.

The job sounded simple enough; however, I was not prepared to do such a difficult task. As you know, roses have long, thorny branches. After my first day, I had little scratches all over my arms. The pain put me in tears.

Mom was upset and said she was going to call to complain that they didn't tell me to wear long sleeves to cover up. I told her not to call. I was determined to prove to everyone that I was ready to work.

My dad gave me an old, long-sleeved dress shirt to wear. This did the trick. It protected my arms and I continued to scratch rosebushes.

My brother, I, and the other kids who were rosebush scratchers tackled the rows together. We moved down the beds in unison. At some point, I felt that we were moving too slowly. I picked up my pace and ended up being half a row ahead of the others. They couldn't believe how fast I was going. I was a machine and I was very proud of myself.

I smiled when I looked back and saw the big boss observing from the end of the beds. I thought, "Wow, he must be so impressed with me! I am so much faster than the rest." I knew he wouldn't regret hiring such a young kid.

I learned a valuable lesson that summer: Impressions are a matter of your frame of reference.

When we got our first paychecks, I eagerly opened mine and noticed that I was being paid twenty-five cents an hour less than the others. But how could this be!? I worked nearly twice as fast as they did.

I walked up to my boss and asked why. He said that when he observed me, I was always half a row behind the others. I was shocked and told him that they were slower and I was half a row ahead of them, not behind.

He didn't believe me and kept my pay where it was. I was upset but undeterred, and I continued working for him for the rest of the summer. I was happy that I was making money and proud of how hard I was working. I returned the following summer to continue that job.

When the job ended, there were still two weeks left of summer break. I wasn't ready to stop working or earning money.

My parents had some friends come over for dinner. They owned a peach farm as well as chickens. We discussed my employment experience and they were very impressed. I asked if I could work for them for the rest of the summer. They agreed and I continued earning money by packing peaches to be shipped to grocery stores. This work was much easier!

I worked exclusively on the peach farm the following summer. I had three years of earnings saved at this point and refused to spend a penny. I was content to just save.

The following year, we moved to another city, which ended my opportunity to work on farms. By this time, I knew that I could not sit at home and do nothing during the summer. I asked my dad what I could do for work.

Dad replied, "Well, you can come work at the University." He was the vice-president of Finance.

"University? I'm too young to be a professor." I was only fourteen years old. Dad laughed and said that he could get me a job working on the maintenance crew. Cool! What does maintenance do? Dad replied, "Whatever they tell you to do."

I was nearly fifteen when I started working maintenance at the university. My job mainly consisted of keeping the eighty acres cut and trimmed. It was hard work, but I got to drive tractors and lawnmowers. I loved it!

Everyone around the university was impressed with me and my work ethic. That opportunity led to others, as I was asked to work in the janitorial department when it was raining. I also got invited by the cafeteria to work evenings and weekends to cater for events.

I worked as much as I could, still saving every single penny.

People began asking me what I planned to do with all my money. My reply was, "I want to buy a house as soon as I can." I never wanted to pay rent or throw money away to a landlord and have nothing to show for it.

I continued working at the university for nine years. I ended up enrolling there in the Fine Arts program. I worked during all five years of my education. I did anything I could, including taking security shifts during the holidays when no one wanted to work. I loved working and making double-time earnings on holidays. And yes, I kept saving.

Find a way to hustle and save to begin your real estate investing journey.

Key Reader Takeaways

Though I didn't know what my goal was at the time, I knew that I wanted to work hard and save as much money as I could.

To enter the world of real estate investing, you must have goals. You also must save as much money as you can.

If you are young and can pull this off while you have little to no expenses, great! If you are established in life and have expenses, you must have the savings mindset. Hustle! Do whatever you can to get ahead.

You may have to work so hard that you miss out on opportunities that your friends get to enjoy. But, at age sixty-five, when everyone else is still working, you will be able to reap the benefits of your hard work and enjoy early retirement.

Keep your eyes on the prize.

True to my word, I bought my first house at age twenty-one. I had just finished my second year of university. The next chapter discusses my first investment property.

CHAPTER 3

MY FIRST INVESTMENT PROPERTY

I never wavered from my goal of home ownership. My years of hard work and savings paid off and I was finally able to realize my dream. After living in the campus residence for two years, I bought my first house.

This was the moment. A lifetime (nine years) of working, saving, and sacrificing all my free time was about to pay off. I was ready to search for my first home. I was in for big changes that year. It was 1992. I was twenty-one years old and about to get married. I thought this was the perfect time to put my plan of home ownership in place.

My parents did offer some guidance and helped me get an appointment with the bank. The bank looked over my finances and decided that, because I work so hard all year round, they would factor as if I were consistently employed, despite that I was still in university full time. Clearly, something was in my favor because they did pre-approve me to buy a $120,000 home. I can't recall how much money I had at that time, but it was at least enough for the 5 percent down payment.

The search was on. My parents came along with my fiancée and I as we looked at house after house. One realtor mistook my youth for ignorance and thought they could pawn a derelict property off on me. I went to an open house and this realtor said, "Hey, I have the perfect property for you. Why don't you meet me there after the open house."

Great! I thought. I drove to the address and got out of my car. The house looked okay from the outside, but when I got inside, the walls had holes, the house smelled, it was dirty, and there were stains everywhere. It looked like the antics of the coyote and roadrunner had taken place. It seemed like a war zone. I took one look at the agent and told him off. "How dare you show me a property like this!" I turned and left.

In retrospect, the derelict home would have likely been a great purchase as an investment property. Some value-added renovations would have paid off by increasing the equity and value of the property. Having said that, my goal at that time was not to become a real estate investor. I just wanted to buy a home for me. The agent should have realized I was not a real estate investor and thought twice about showing me such a property.

After the showing, I went home feeling discouraged and told my parents how disappointed I was with the house I'd just seen. They felt bad for me but said it was part of the home-buying process. Finding the right home takes time. They suggested that my fiancée and I use a family friend who was a realtor.

Before the days of the internet, realtors had access to information that we take for granted today. He called me up and said he already made an appointment at a house that had just come up on the market. He had a feeling about this house and wanted us to see it before anyone else. I was impressed and happy that I didn't have to look at more battle zone properties.

When we arrived for the appointment, we were completely blown away. It was a one-and-a-half-story wartime house. It had a large extra-wide driveway, a fenced yard, a shed, great neighbors, and was in a great part of town. When we stepped inside, our jaws hit the floor. The house had been completely remodeled. It was an open concept, something I had never seen in any home I had been in. There were decorative mirrors on the walls. These design elements were not part of my frugal Dutch upbringing. The staircase was in the center of the house and was a central design feature. The steps were slats of wood with no faces. You could see the open space right between them. I had never seen such a form or function. The upstairs had two bedrooms, one on either side of the staircase. On the main floor, at the back of the living room, a sliding glass door opened into a large office or den. A door at the back of the den led to a landing that showed a separate entry to the side of the house. This was the laundry room. In the basement, we were shocked to find a two-bedroom apartment.

We were blown away with this house. The basement apartment was a foreign concept to me. I had never considered having tenants. Our realtor explained that the apartment could be rented to college or university students to cover the bulk of the mortgage payments. This place was too good to be true.

We asked how much for this dream home. The realtor replied, "$135,000!" My bones turned to Jell-O. I'm sure my posture collapsed and my face sank. Why would the realtor show me something outside of my budget? He explained that, though it was out of my pre-approval, the apartment would make it much cheaper to own.

Okay . . . great! But how do I convince the bank to give me more money? We left the house with mixed emotions. The home was perfect, and yet not meant to be. I was deflated by the process once again.

After we got home, I couldn't find my parents. They had disappeared into their bedroom. A short while later, they came downstairs and said they thought the house was perfect and that I likely wouldn't find anything better than that. I agreed, but reminded them that it was $15,000 beyond my price range. They looked at each other and smirked and then looked at me and said, "We want you to have that house and we are going to help you out."

I said, "You're going to give me $15,000?"

They responded with, "No."

I looked at them, confused, and then they said they were going to give me $30,000.

What? Really? Why? They said I had been working so hard and that, in reality, that house would be cheaper because of the basement apartment. They also said that they didn't want me to have a high-ratio mortgage. When homebuyers provide less than a 20 percent down payment, they pay Canadian Mortgage and Housing Corporation (CMHC) insurance that costs thousands. (Dutch people do not like to waste money). They told me to call the realtor and have him put an offer in right away, and after a couple of back-and-forth singings, we ended up with an accepted offer of $131,000. I was ecstatic!

I found two guys at my university who said they would love to rent my apartment for $600 a month. I agreed, and they moved in shortly after we took possession. Could life get any more perfect? Not having a crystal ball, I would never have predicted that it would all come crashing down. More about that in the next chapter.

Success is within your grasp!

KEY READER TAKEAWAYS

Hard work will eventually pay off. It takes time to find the right deal, and you need the right people and support network.

Not everyone's parents get it or are encouraging, but don't let that deter you. The $30,000 from my parents was a great help but, ultimately, there are creative ways to source extra money to buy a property that's just outside your budget. Or you can wait. A property within your budget will eventually come along.

Some people use a line of credit for part or all of the down payment. I have even heard of people leveraging credit cards in order to get into the market; however, I do not condone this due to the high interest rates that credit cards charge.

Another creative method includes selling personal items that you really don't need. Examine what is more important for you. Would you rather own a home, a boat, or a car? I believe it is better to get into the real estate market and buy peripheral items when you have your first property locked down. If you choose to house hack, you can write off a portion of your expenses, which can include some of the costs associated with owning and operating a vehicle. Speak to a certified accountant for more information on tax benefits.

Other sources of creative financing include borrowing money from family, as I did. I paid my parents back years later when I sold that property.

Look for opportunity wherever you can. That basement apartment allowed me to get the house of my dreams and supplemented my expenses in a big way. I was house hacking before the term existed. I highly encourage anyone looking for their first property to house hack (more on this topic later).

You can take the leap of faith to realize your dreams.

CHAPTER 4

THE WANDERING YEARS

1992 was a big year for me. I bought my first home and got married. I was in a living fairy tale with my happily ever after. I thought life couldn't get any better. I was doing what you were supposed to do: Buy a house, get married, have a child, and be a provider. I accomplished most of this by age twenty-one. By twenty-four, I was a father. I graduated from university and had a huge head-start on life.

Despite the best-laid plans, life will never unfold and work out the way you expect it to. Little did I know that everything was about to change. Without going into a lot of detail, my marriage came to an end. I moved back into my parents' house with no direction and a lot of repressed emotions.

I came close to losing the house I had worked so hard for. It nearly went into foreclosure. I managed to avoid that and held on to the house. My basement tenants moved out and I was left with this asset that I wasn't prepared to live in. I ended up renting the house to a family. Their rent was just a little more than what the mortgage cost. I was living with my parents with no full-time job, no direction, and no ambition.

Eventually, I found work in the world of business. I worked for a couple of years for a start-up phone company. I learned a lot about business, but it wasn't my passion. I wanted to do something that tapped into my creativity. I decided to leave the phone company to pursue an education in the world of advertising and design. I finished a two-year college program and took some odd jobs to pay the bills before getting hired as a part-time graphic designer.

In between some contract gigs at some boutique design firms, I took on factory jobs and computer sales jobs. I did well but, again, that wasn't what I wanted to do. It wasn't my passion, and it didn't feed my soul. I kept searching for work in the world of advertising but wasn't finding much.

In Canada, times were tough for people with white-collar jobs. At the time, the best and brightest minds were leaving for the United States. This was known as the Great Brain Drain. I decided, what have I got to lose? I grabbed my portfolio and drove across the border.

Things changed right away for me. I actually got call-backs when I applied for jobs. I ended up getting hired right away at an ad agency in Pittsburgh. I was doing what I loved as a designer and art director!

While I was interviewing for jobs in Pittsburgh, I did an interview at a college for a faculty of graphic design position. I didn't put much thought into the interview. I treated it more like practice for other interviews. Several months after I took my job as a designer/art director, to my surprise, I got an offer to teach graphic design. I decided to take a year off from advertising to experience the world of teaching. That one-year step away from being an art director turned into two and then three years. My life and career had once again taken a detour. I committed to being a college professor. My career had direction and I was excelling once again.

I decided that I was going to make the United States my permanent home and decided to sell my house in Canada.

Life throws changes at you all the time. I became discontent living in the US and decided to move back to Canada. I was hired as a professor of advertising at a college in eastern Ontario. I moved to a small town that I knew nothing about. It had charm and offered a great quality of life for me and my son. I seemed to know right away that I was in the place I would call home and would live there until I retired.

I was back in the mode of doing what you were supposed to do. I had a career. I worked at a great place. I lived in a wonderful community. I wanted to buy a house, but that was easier said than done.

Since I had been living outside of Canada for a few years, I had no credit when I moved back. Despite having all the security of being a full-time professor, I couldn't get a bank to finance me to buy a home. In fact, I couldn't even get a credit card. I rented for the first year or so. I was not happy. Renting was never something I wanted to do.

Enough time passed that the bank finally gave me a credit card. They were only going to approve a $500 limit. How embarrassing! My students were getting approved for credit cards with higher limits.

I guess the past was haunting me. My first house nearly fell into repossession, but I avoided that at the last minute. For those who don't know, if you miss a couple of payments, the bank begins the process to seize the property from you. While living at my parents' house, I was not making my mortgage payments. The state of my life and the depression caused by my marriage collapsing removed my care and desire to make the payments. When I received the notice of repossession, I went straight to the bank and paid all the money owing and got my asset back. Then I came to my senses and agreed to find a tenant for the entire house.

I had a vague idea of how credit and credit ratings worked. My bank advisor encouraged me to purchase essential things on the card and then pay it off in full every month. It was extremely important that I never carried a balance. Not only would this incur high interest charges, but it would also not help me dig myself out of the credit hole I was in.

I heeded her advice and stuck to my guns. To ensure that I never overspent on my credit card, I devised a plan: I opened a second bank account. Each time I made a purchase, I transferred that amount from my checking account to my savings account. I pretended like my savings account didn't exist. A couple of days before my credit card bill was due, I transferred the full amount from my savings to my checking account and paid the credit card bill.

I felt quite proud that I was managing my finances and living within my means with my measly $500 credit card limit.

A year later, I approached my bank advisor and asked if I could get pre-approved for a loan to buy a house. She ran my credit score and I had completely turned it around. My credit wasn't perfect, but it was way better than it had been. I had a 620 credit score. Not stellar, but not horrible. She did say, however, that if I were approved for a mortgage, I would likely need a co signer.

How did I go from getting approved to buy my first home in 1992 to the banks being apprehensive about me in 2004? I was an adult with a fantastic career and yet I still needed help from Mom and Dad. I spoke with them about it. I made my case about how secure I was in my position and how I hated the fact that I had to rent. I assured them that I would be responsible and not mess this up. They agreed to co sign so I could buy a home. I found a nice three-bedroom home and moved out of my two-bedroom apartment.

I guess my dad decided that there should be more positive movement in my life. He knew I had always loved the water and longed to own a boat. A colleague at the college told me he was selling his 30-foot sailboat. I mentioned it to my dad and he replied, "Then buy it!" I said I just bought the house and didn't have money for a boat. He said, "I didn't ask you to pay for it. I'll buy it, you take care of it and all the associated expenses, and I will share it with you."

Wow! How could I resist that offer? So, I purchased a 1971 Grampian 30 sailboat. It was beautiful! But where would I keep it? My colleague who sold me the boat (and became a very good friend) told me it only cost a couple hundred bucks to join the yacht club and they had city-run docks. My buddy gave me the contact information for the City so I could secure a slip.

It was amazing how life had turned around in such a short time. The best thing about joining the yacht club was that it became a great place to network and meet new people. Most of the members were older. They instantly embraced having a young new member. I was introduced to quite a few people, but I became quite close with one couple in particular. They were even younger than me. They owned a small sailboat, a Tanser 22, and he shared ownership of a duplex with his brother. With our shared interest, we hit it off.

I enjoyed the process of looking for a house and checking listings. Something inside me kept me looking at what was on the market. Eventually, a house caught my eye. It wasn't much bigger than what I was living in now, but there were a couple of other things going for it. It was a waterfront property! It had a finished basement with a bar and a separate entrance in the backyard. I saw all of this and thought, "Holy cow!" I could put a wall up and wire in a stove and voilà! A two-bedroom basement apartment! I thought about how that had worked for me in my first home and how it could work again. I could enjoy my love of the water year-round.

It was November, the market was dead, and this house kept dropping in price. I got excited and made an appointment with my bank advisor to ask if there was any way I could get approved, even though I just bought a house earlier that year. This waterfront home cost significantly more; however, I explained to the bank manager that, after factoring in the income from the basement apartment, I would end up living cheaper.

She crunched the numbers and agreed. She ran my credit score and was extremely excited to tell me that I no longer required a co signer. Not even a year had passed since my parents were required to co sign for me. I couldn't believe it!

I told my parents about my plan and they were amazed that I was able to pull this off so quickly. I think they also wanted the security of knowing that they were not financially tied to my mortgage.

I had a realtor come over and do a market assessment of my home. To my surprise, it had increased in value. I couldn't believe that the waterfront home was so close to becoming a reality. I booked a viewing and soon realized why it wasn't selling. Yes, the market was crap this close to Christmas, but the main factor was that the present homeowner was a hoarding chain-smoker. I asked why she was selling the house and found out that she was an American who moved to Canada and bought the house on a whim. She had no legal status in Canada and had been given an order to move back to the US.

My agent looked at me with a grimace on her face. I said, "I can't believe it!" I think she thought I was going to comment on the horrible condition of the house. I repeated, "I can't believe I can buy a waterfront home for an amazing price!"

I looked past all the deficiencies, which were merely cosmetic. The current owner was between a rock and a hard place. I put in a major low-ball offer and, after some back and forth, she accepted a loss. Her misfortune was my gain.

I listed my house and prayed to God that it would sell. I ended up getting an offer $10,000 more than what I had paid for the place less than a year earlier. The stars were aligned. I was going to have just enough money from the sale to finance the down payment and closing costs of the waterfront property.

Life was finally on track. I felt like I was going in the direction I had been back in 1992. I was once again house hacking to upgrade my lifestyle.

Learn to filter the distractions. Make a plan and stay focused!

KEY READER TAKEAWAYS

First, life will never take the path you plan. You will hit stumbling blocks as well as opportunities. Take the time you need to heal and take the opportunities that are presented to you. If you stumble in life, there is always time to get back up. Life can be hard, but don't let it be debilitating. When you crash, there will always be a time to rise.

Second, do not despair if you have bad credit. It is manageable. Put the strategies in place that I used. I had the second-lowest credit rating possible and turned it around in just one year. It takes focus, determination, and strategy. I did benefit from having my parents as co signers, and if you can get this kind of assistance, great! It isn't necessary though. A few more months of following my plan to use my credit card and pay it off each month would have yielded the same result. I was just impatient and didn't want to wait.

Look for the less-than-desirable path when you want to buy a home at a good price. Look past cosmetic flaws. Consider how to house hack to make your dream a reality. Have an open mind.

Lastly, don't be afraid to gather intel and leverage it to your advantage. The illegal immigrant's misfortune became my gain. If I hadn't taken advantage of that intel, someone else would have.

It's never too late to change your situation.

Life on the water was amazing. I always described it as living on vacation. This new home cost more than my previous one, so I had to increase my income. Working full time as a professor meant I had no time or energy to take on another job. I needed to get back to my roots and begin house hacking.

CHAPTER 5

THE RETURN TO FOCUS AND THE LEAP OF FAITH

I absolutely loved living on the water. The house was on a river canal where I watched yachts go by all day. The house, though dated, was amazing. It had a boathouse and steps down to the water. Three bedrooms, a bathroom, an eat-in kitchen, a living room, and sunroom made up the upstairs. The finished basement had two bedrooms, a bathroom, a large living room, a bar/kitchenette, and a walk-out to the backyard. This basement was a goldmine and required very little work to convert into a separate apartment.

I had done it for my first home in order to afford it, and now it was time to do it again to make my waterfront home more affordable. It was time to house hack.

Just like my first house, this one was ideally set up with a separate entrance and plenty of space for someone to live below. There were just a few things missing. The bar was gaudy, large and dated. It had to go. But what do

I replace it with? I couldn't afford a new kitchen. This is where my creativity came into play.

On my way into town, I stopped at a local hardware store to look around. There was a long narrow piece of countertop at a massive discount. Someone must have returned it or had it custom ordered and it arrived in the wrong specs. I snatched it up cheap, which appealed to my Dutch sensibilities. I continued on down to my favorite Canadian big-box store. This store was known for having clearance items as well as 70 percent-off sales all the time. Low and behold, I found a couple of low square shelves and thought, this could work. I bought a couple of casters and figured I could improve the shelves by making them mobile. I could then affix the countertop to the beautiful square shelves and have a movable counter that could be more versatile in the space. This would be way better than the massive, ugly old wooden bar that I had just ripped out. It fit perfectly in the space. It looked sleek and custom, and the best part was, it cost me barely any money.

The only thing that was missing to make the kitchenette complete was a stove. I reached out to my buddy whom I met at the yacht club. He was an electrician, and he had no problem installing the stove for me. Another good friend from the college was handy with building. He had helped a few people build some nice decks. I told him about my plan for the basement and what I needed to build a wall to separate the house into two units. He instantly said, "I'll help you!"

He came over and the wall went up with soundproof insulation in just one day. Now I was off to the races. As soon as the wall was complete, I had a young couple move in. They were paying a good chunk of my mortgage. Life was great!

My friend who helped me build the wall was going to the popular watering hole and suggested I join him. In the neighboring town, this bar was the place for professionals to hang out on a Friday. Before long, I was somewhat a happy-hour regular. I met some great people and continued my networking journey. Two people ended up being very influential. They were both full-time landlords. I was amazed someone could make a living as a landlord and didn't do it as a side gig.

I continued hanging out at the bar in the next town. It was close to the college where I worked. It was great to hang out with all kinds of professional people. The landlords I met were both very interesting. One was a single mother who owned two sixplexes. In one of her properties, she combined two of her units and lived in a nice, large space. The remaining units completely funded her lifestyle. She was able to buy a Harley and go biking with her friends and travel whenever she wanted to. I had so much respect for her.

The other landlord friend was a single guy. He was on a whole other level. He owned over 200 units! This guy came in every time to the bar excited for the next deal he landed. I was shocked that someone could own that much property. I inquired as to how he did it. He told me about leveraging. Borrowing against the value of one property to finance the down payment on another.

These two became my new heroes. They both kept encouraging me to get into the property game in a serious way. I kept wanting to do it but was really scared to take that step.

There came a time when my one landlord friend mentioned that her brother had a sevenplex in town that he was considering selling, and that I could do an off-market deal and save tens of thousands of dollars by purchasing it from him.

I was so excited to begin my financial journey as a serious landlord. I discussed it with my then girlfriend and she hated the idea. She said she didn't want to move into a place that we had to share with tenants. I explained that it would be a short-term thing until I could leverage that property and buy something else. She was adamant that it was not for her.

I didn't make that deal and I have always regretted it. Things with my girlfriend didn't work out and I regretted allowing someone who wasn't contributing financially to the relationship to control what I did with my money and future. To this day, when I drive by that sevenplex, a little piece of me sighs and thinks of what could have been.

Not making the move on the sevenplex stagnated me somewhat. I kept hearing about the lives that my landlord friends had and kept yearning to live that experience.

When they found out my relationship ended, they were very supportive. I did lament to my friend and her brother that I didn't buy his sevenplex. The siblings kept pushing me to make the move to become a serious real estate investor.

I allowed my fears, anxieties, and external pressures to control my decision-making process. Indeed, my own family members, who have always been very supportive, discouraged the idea of real estate investing. They felt it was too risky. It required too much capital, and they didn't like the idea of leveraging one property to purchase another. I let the external naysayers get to me for the next two years.

I'd dragged my heels for long enough. My landlord friends were doing great. Their real estate investing gave them the freedom to live life on their own terms. I was doing great too, but the reality is, working for someone else will never make you rich. Nor will it offer you security for your future. Yes, I had a great job as a professor. I was making great money and had lots of time off and an amazing pension and benefit package, but something inside of me kept saying it wasn't enough.

The catalyst came when we were about to go on strike. I suddenly realized that my cushy, secure job wasn't all that I thought it was. I was suddenly scared. How would I pay all my bills with only strike pay? When the strike was averted at the last minute, I breathed a sigh of relief. Right after that deep exhale, I knew it was time to make a change in my life. I could no longer have all my eggs in one basket. Now was the time. I needed to take the plunge into real estate investing.

I am a planner and a dreamer. I thought, if it all works out, great! I'll be able to take an early retirement. If it all goes to hell in a handbasket and I lose my shirt, then I will have to work and retire at the same age as everyone else. This was a risk I had to take.

I began looking at properties for sale on the realtor's website. A property caught my eye. It was a semi-detached duplex and it had an open house that day. I drove into town and fell in love with the place. It had always been owned by families that occupied both units. It had never been used as a rental. It was built in 1865, two years older than Canada, but you wouldn't have known it. Its owners clearly loved it from the day it was built.

I had to have it. I didn't have an agent of my own, so I made all my inquiries with the listing agent. She was quite good at separating her roles in representing both the buyer and the seller. She did tell me that the only issue was that an offer had already been accepted. My heart sank until she said, "but . . . it's 'bumpable.'" I inquired as to what that meant. She said that the current offer was conditional on the sale of two other properties and that it didn't look like either of those properties would sell in time.

Once again, I was on fire. I called my bank and asked to have the soonest-available appointment with my mortgage broker. The broker I had dealt with before moved to another bank, but the new broker was really good, too. She saw my vision and helped me explore my options. When we sat down together and went over the numbers, she said I should be approved to buy the property. She explained that I had quite a bit of equity in my waterfront home and that the basement apartment helped with my income calculation.

Then, I had an idea. I thought to myself, if my goal is to start accumulating multiple properties to get ahead and not rely on my job as my only source of income, why should I sell one home to buy two? Why not keep my waterfront home and buy the duplex? So, I asked my mortgage broker if there was a way I could make this happen. She said yes and ordered an appraisal on my waterfront home and an appraisal on the duplex. She asked the appraiser to include what fair-market rent would be on all three places. The duplex had no history of rentals, so there was no record of income to go by.

When the appraisals came in, they were very favorable. My mortgage broker said to go ahead and make an offer on the duplex. I was so excited. I called my agent and told her I wanted to offer the full price for the house. Everyone said that was nuts, but the accepted offer needed to be bumped.

It wasn't long before the other buyer withdrew his offer, as he wasn't in a place to firm up the deal. His misfortune became my gain. I got the duplex and had all my conditions met.

I found tenants who would pay me top dollar to live on the water, provided that they could have the entire place, so, I removed the wall that was built a couple of years earlier. I moved into one side of the duplex and rented out the other side. Now I was making a lot of money passively. I was earning about 60 percent of my professor salary. I was on track to financial freedom.

Find yourself good tenants. This takes time and effort, but the process is worth it.

Key Reader Takeaways

Some things I want you to be able to do:

Be creative. Don't just take things at face value. Learn to troubleshoot and problem solve by thinking outside of the box. Some of the best solutions can be achieved through unconventional ways. This is true not only in looking at how a space can be utilized or optimized, but it also relates to how you strategize the deals, financing, and your personal life.

When assessing the layout of a home, look for where a wall could go up or a new exterior door could be installed to create another rental unit.

Strategizing a deal doesn't have to be as simple as saving up for the down payment and applying for a loan to cover the rest. Consider how you could leverage alternate sources of financing. If you already own a property, you can tap into the equity of that property and use a home equity line of credit for the down payment. You could also ask the seller to consider financing a portion of the purchase. This is called a vender take-back or VTB.

With respect to your personal life, you can get creative in how you choose to use a new property. If you move into the property, you can get away with less of a down payment. Often it is only 5 percent of the purchase price. Being willing to move could help you get ahead faster and for less out-of-pocket money. Really, the creative options are endless and are only limited by your imagination.

Align your goals. Make sure you and your partner (if you have one) are like-minded. This will not only prove to be of benefit in your relationship, but also in your financial endeavors. Be honest with yourself about who you have in your life. Are you holding out for what could be, or are you both aligned and motivated to get ahead, personally and professionally?

Network. Find groups, service clubs, or a pub, etc. where you can meet different people. Not only is it good for your soul to socialize and meet other professional people, but you never know how that connection may benefit you. We all come from different backgrounds with different areas of expertise and skill sets. Be open to sharing yours and don't be afraid to reach out to tap into the abilities of a friend.

When it comes to real estate investing, double network and educate yourself. In other words, start by watching YouTube videos. Find an individual who is into real estate investing. Pick their brain. Ask them about how they got to where they are in the business. Ask them about their struggles and regrets. Find more real estate investors to learn from. We all have our own stories of our successes and failures, and each one of us is willing to share. Get involved with a local landlord group. Get involved with online discussion groups. Don't waste your money on conventions and seminars (these didn't exist when I was starting out, nor did YouTube).

There are advantages to using a realtor to represent both your interests as a buyer and seller. Though agents need to maintain professionalism and abide by ethics, they will still push harder for your deal to close when they know they will earn commission from both sides. They have a vested interest in seeing the sale through. I have landed many deals using this tactic.

Lastly, do not delay. Get in the game. Take the leap of faith. Set a goal and then exceed it. I wasted two years dragging my heels before getting into the game. I was excited about it, and it was a burning passion that was being suppressed beneath the surface. Too many people hold back because of their fear of the unknown. If you are still young, get into the game ASAP. If you are not young, it is never too late.

Now is the time.

Once again, I felt that life was complete. I was finally getting ahead. My money was now working for me rather than me working for my money. I didn't think it could get any better. Who knew what could happen in only a few months?

CHAPTER 6
FOR THE LOVE OF LEVERAGING

What can I say? I pulled it off. I did what I thought was impossible. I bought a duplex without having to sell my waterfront home. I had leveraged that home to make affording the duplex possible. I achieved a larger source of passive income through having two rental properties in one move. The best part is, I did this all with "other people's money."

Other people's money may be a term you've heard before but likely don't fully understand or believe. How is it possible that someone can get ahead while other people pay for it? Surely something must be wrong or illegal. It all boils down to leveraging.

Here is a brief lesson on how leveraging works: In the case of my waterfront home, I had lived in it for a few years. This allowed me to make a bit of a dent in the principal amount that I owed on my mortgage. Each month you make a mortgage payment, the bulk of it goes toward the interest and the remainder goes toward the principal. The combined interest and principal payments are the amount you owe to complete the purchase of a home (usually spread over twenty-five years). The amount of the house that you actually own is known as the equity. The equity is an invisible (artificial) amount of money that is determined by the amount you've paid off on your loan and the amount that your property has increased in value since the purchase date. To summarize, the mortgage is the debt made up of principal and interest. The equity is the amount paid off plus the value added over time.

It is important to understand this concept and how it works. There are ways to fast track the increase in value of a home. That is through what you do to improve the property. When I bought the waterfront home, it was owned by a hoarding chain smoker. The property did not show well, and this definitely affected how the property's value was appraised. While I lived there, I made improvements to the property. I cleaned it up, painted everything, including the kitchen cabinets, and installed new hardware. I made improvements to the landscaping, gardening, decks, fences, and the shed. This improved the curb appeal. I hadn't spent a lot of money on these projects, but I did put a lot of elbow grease in to make the home better.

This investment of time and energy worked out for me in the bank's appraisal. They determined that the property had significantly increased in value and therefore gave the bank confidence in lending me more money to purchase the duplex.

When you look at what I had done, I had signed my name to a piece of property and did not pull any money out of my own bank account to close the deal. The funds that allowed me to make the move to the new property were magically derived out of thin air based on the value of the equity in my waterfront home. I loved this concept! I used the bank's money to get ahead. I had set up the waterfront house as a rental that not only paid the entire mortgage, taxes, and insurance, but also generated a bit of a profit (cash flow) each month for me to use.

I also set up the other side of the duplex as a rental and this paid 100 percent of the costs of that property. I was now living for free. This went beyond the house hacking that I had done with basement apartments up until this point. This concept is known as other people's money.

I was so excited when I went back to the bar in town to proclaim what I had done to my landlord friends. They revelled in my success and said, "Well, now that you've gotten a taste, you need to keep going!" I was shocked. Really? So soon? I had only just closed on the duplex and moved in. My one landlord friend with over 200 units said that, once it starts, you can snowball the effect rather quickly. I was fascinated and excited at the prospect of being able to pull this all off again. It wasn't long before I pulled out my computer and began looking at property listings on the realtor's website.

Suddenly, something caught my eye. A gorgeous house in a nice part of town. It had five bedrooms, three bathrooms, an eat-in kitchen, a separate dining room, and a finished basement which included two bedrooms, a bathroom, a gorgeous, over-sized laundry room, two storage rooms, an immense family room with a fireplace, a bonus cold-storage room, and a large built-in hot rock sauna that seated six. This sauna was just like the ones you see at the YMCA. I couldn't believe it. It was only $5,000 more than what I had paid for the duplex.

I contacted my mortgage specialist at my bank and made an appointment with her. I asked if there was any way I could pull off purchasing this property without having to sell the waterfront home or the duplex. She was shocked. It had been only a month since I moved into the duplex. She said, "Let me run the numbers and call the underwriters and I'll get back to you."

A few days passed before my mortgage broker contacted me and said, "I pulled some strings and really went to bat for you. I finally secured an approval; however, the bank wants you to put 5 percent down of your own money this time. And . . . there's another catch . . . The bank says you cannot do this anymore. This is the final time they will allow you to only put 5 percent down on a house. So, you are going to have to cool it after this."

"No problem," I said. I just want to pull this off.

After having owned the duplex for only four months, I ended up closing on the other home. There wasn't much equity to leverage in the duplex since I had just closed on it, but what the bank did do was look at the increase in revenue. Now I was going to have three rental properties that would pay for my fourth. This factored into my income calculation that allowed me to get approved.

My family and friends thought I was nuts. I was now in debt an insane amount of money. Having said that, I was earning more money each month than what my expenses amounted to. I was continuing to cash flow. The best part is, I no longer had to rely on my job as my only source of income. If my union ever voted to strike, I knew I could float all my expenses. I thought I had it made in the shade . . . all thanks to other people's money.

Life just kept getting better and better. I rekindled my relationship with the woman who was against the purchase of the sevenplex. We moved in together into the new house. I thought, perhaps now she will see how good it is to have rental properties and, just maybe, she would be more supportive. This ended up being a poor move. It didn't last long. Within a year, I found that I was trying to force a situation that was never meant to work out. I determined that the relationship was doomed.

Being the kindhearted guy that I am, I offered to let her stay in the house as a tenant. I would let her and her three kids rent the upper half of the house and I would wall off the basement so that it could be a separate apartment.

I called my electrician friend from the yacht club and asked if he would install a stove line. Within a couple of weeks, the wall was built, the stove line was installed, I purchased a stove and fridge, and found a new tenant. Once again, I made an incredible cash flow where one hadn't existed before.

On paper, this looked amazing (financially). I now had income from five different units. These doors made more than what I earned as a full-time professor. By all rights, I was rich but I was also homeless. The irony was that I owned five homes but didn't have a place to live. What was I to do? The banks were clear that I couldn't borrow any more money to buy another property. A new house just for me was out of the question.

I called my good friend from the bar. She was the one who owned 11 units. I asked her if she had any vacancy. She was shocked but not surprised that my relationship ended yet again. She told me that she happened to have a one-bedroom apartment available in the fiveplex she lived in. She offered it to me on the spot and, without hesitation, I took her up on the offer. She knew enough about me to know I was not a risky tenant. She didn't even ask for my financials, as she knew that I made more than enough money to cover the rent. She actually helped me move all my belongings into the apartment. We became very close after that. What an incredible friend she ended up being!

KEY READER TAKEAWAYS

What I hope you got out of this chapter was to recognize that money is a game. It is a game you need to learn to play. Everything I had done up to this point was using the art of leveraging and maximizing income in order to live off of other people's money. I hadn't used my own money to accumulate these income properties. In fact, I wasn't even using my own money to pay for the one-bedroom apartment I was renting.

Here is a good lesson for you to learn: Money doesn't exist. In fact, the way money is created is through debt. When you borrow money from the bank to buy a property, they are only required to have 1/10 the amount of funds in deposit of what they actually lend. To put it simply, to borrow $100,000, the bank only has to have funds of $10,000. The remaining $90,000 doesn't exist. It was created out of thin air. It is a debt that is owed on an unreal amount of money. The reality is, every time someone borrows money from the banks, you are creating money out of thin air. Sounds like a game now, doesn't it? Learn to play this game.

Money is an artificial abstract concept that doesn't exist. In 1971, the United States Federal Reserve went off of the gold standard. Up until that point, money was tied to gold: $1 = $1 of gold that was locked in a vault. Since this point, fiat currency became the new form of money. It is not tied to anything. It is simply printed as needed. This continual printing reduces the value of the dollar. This is known as inflation. If you leave your money in the bank for one year, it will be worth less money due to inflation. You need to see money as an artificial construct that is fluid. The more debt that gets created, the more money comes into existence. Study and learn as much about this as you can, and you will then master what they do not teach in schools. You will think of money differently and you will see the game of finance as something that needs to be played in order to get ahead. If you don't play, you can't win.

I have spoken before about being creative. It is important to apply that creativity when looking at the potential of a property. Look for things like separate entrances. Is there a space where a wall could go up to turn a single family home into a duplex? Is there a separate bathroom and kitchen? Are there or could there be separate bedrooms? What is the full, unrealized income potential?

I mentioned previously the importance of networking. This is not only useful as a guide in realizing your real estate goals but also as an individual. My network of friends was very supportive in encouraging me to continue my investing journey and when I needed them as counsel and support on personal matters. These friends became a lifeline. Maintain a good group of solid, professional friends. The value of a good network of friends is irreplaceable!

Do what is best for you. I held on to an on-again/off-again relationship for far too long. This held me back personally and professionally. Your partner needs to be aligned with you on all levels. Expecting that they are, when every indication is that they aren't, means you are holding onto a dream of what could be rather than the reality of what is. I am not suggesting that you be so quick to throw in the towel with a difficult relationship. Obviously, you know deep down if the effort is worth it. Having said that, if you feel like you are making most or all the effort in the relationship, then it is doomed to fail. In my case, we were too different and were not aligned at all in our personal and professional desires and goals. This is a sure sign that it is time to cut ties and move on.

It's fair to say that life for me at this point was the best of times and the worst of times. I had an on-again/off-again personal relationship and, as it turned out, I was about to realize that I had an on-again/off-again relationship with my properties.

CHAPTER 7
BOOMERANG-ANG-ANG

I was enjoying the single life. I was living very cheaply in a one-bedroom apartment. I had a great social and dating life going on. I was earning great money from my job and my rentals. This all changed when one of my tenants in the duplex gave notice to move out. This put me in a bit of a bind. I was about to lose a significant amount of income.

Since I was living in a rental, I considered moving back to the duplex. But what was a single guy to do with a four-bedroom duplex? After crunching the numbers, the answer was quite clear. It was time to house hack once again.

I received a call one day from my insurance company. They had sent me a letter that was returned. They didn't know I had moved into a rental. When they heard this, they told me that I had to live in at least one of my properties to maintain my insurance. They said that they were going to drop me and cancel my policy in thirty days. I was stunned. What difference did it make? I was still making my payments. I needed to really think about what I had to do.

I loved living in the one-bedroom apartment on my own. I also loved living so close to a good friend. But, when I looked at the numbers, I realized I could make nearly twice as much money by renting out individual rooms and still have a place to live. It didn't take me long to decide. I could earn even more money and maintain my insurance policy.

I pulled my friend aside and thanked her for being there for me and for giving me a place to live when I needed it. I explained that I was in a bit of a predicament with the upcoming vacancy in my duplex. I was going to lose a significant amount of income and it seemed to make more sense for me to live there. I gave her my notice, she understood, and I moved back into my duplex.

There's something that has always made me feel so good about that duplex. I loved living there before and was very excited to move back in. This time, however, I was moving into the side I had not lived in before, so this was kind of new for me, and that made it just a bit more exciting.

I was going to have to house hack again. This time would be different though. I would not have a separate basement apartment to rent out. This time I would have roommates.

It wasn't so bad. I was single, so I didn't need to compromise with a partner. I took the large bedroom on the lower level. The other three bedrooms were upstairs. It would sort of feel like I had my own space, except that the kitchen, living room, and laundry room were all downstairs. I would still be sharing my space with other people.

Since I was a professor at the local college, I knew there was a need for students to have a place to live off campus. I figured that if I could get students in, they would likely be appreciative of the quality home and enjoy living with a professor from the school they attended. I posted an ad online and, before I knew it, all three rooms were filled by great guys. I rented the rooms unfurnished but provided the living room furniture and kitchen table for them to use.

I had not lived with guys like this since I was in university. Now, more than twenty years later, I was living like a college kid again. For the most part, there were no issues. We all got along. They were devoted to their studies and extra-curricular activities. They saw me as a bit of a father figure, which likely contributed to them feeling comfortable being away from home for the first time. Life was great! I was earning more than I had been with the previous tenants, I was no longer paying rent, and I had a place to live. Win! Win! Win!

This living situation went on for the entire first semester (four months). It was great the whole time. Then, my tenants on the other side of the duplex gave their notice. I wasn't concerned, as I had it made the way I was living now. I did, however, think to myself that the other side had an extra bedroom. I could live like this and make more money! Once again, I was going to increase my bottom line.

I sat the guys down and explained that the other side was nicer and had an extra bedroom. I asked if they minded moving across and continuing our living arrangements, apart from bringing one more roommate in. They all were easygoing guys. They said that it wasn't a problem at all.

I couldn't believe how my financial situation was improving again in such a short amount of time. We moved across to the other unit, found another roommate, and I thought it was all amazing.

Not long after living on the other side, I was having issues with my tenants in my waterfront home. They were being difficult. Rent was late, their communication ceased, and then their rent payments ceased altogether. Uh oh! It wasn't looking good. Panic set in and I started losing sleep over it.

I hired a paralegal who specialized in landlord–tenant law. In fact, he only represented landlords. I filed suit to have the tenants evicted. I got my hearing date and was sick to my stomach. When the adjudicator called my case, we looked around the room and the tenants were nowhere to be found. It was all over in a few minutes. I got my eviction order and a judgment for rent arrears.

I kept driving by the property every few days. It was not looking good. Vehicles were still there. Garbage was piling up on the porch and yard. It seemed like I still wasn't going to be able to get rid of them. Thank God I had all the income that I did. I would have lost the house otherwise.

Finally, the days were drawing closer to when the sheriff was to go out to serve and enforce the eviction. I drove out a couple of days before and, low and behold, they were gone.

Thank God. At least I didn't need to escalate things to the level of eviction through the sheriff. This saved me time, a few hundred dollars, and the added stress.

I carefully opened the door and made my way inside. What had they done? There was damage and garbage and even pet messes throughout the home. These people did not treat the home with the love and respect an owner would. I came to realize that this can often be the case with tenants. Some tenants are great and others rent for a reason. I happened to find the ones who didn't care at all about the state of the property.

I made my way down to the boathouse. I went inside and found it entirely full of garbage bags. These tenants did not throw out a single bag since moving in. They just threw them into the boathouse. There were all types of garbage, dirty diapers, and debris. The place had an awful stench.

I was deflated and depressed. How could l this happen? Why would people choose to live like this? Why were they so irresponsible with my property? How could they not meet their obligations of rent and utilities and just abandon such a wonderful place?

I went home and told my roommates what was going on. They could see the stress on my face and body language. They felt really bad for me. I had been such a good guy to them and they hated seeing me taken advantage of like this.

I lamented to a friend about the situation I was in. I told her that the property was left in shambles. It was going to take a long time to fix it up. I explained that, even when it was fixed up, I was concerned about renting to bad tenants like that again. She came up with a solution. She suggested that I should try this new online platform called Airbnb.

"What the heck is that?" I asked.

She said, "It's so amazing! You take photos of your property, do a wonderful writeup for it, and they list it and turn it into a vacation rental, like a hotel. The best part is, you don't get stuck with bad tenants. You can say 'no pets' and charge a damage deposit."

Wow! This was incredible! I will definitely need to get the place fixed up and list it.

I spent all my free time going back and forth from the duplex to my waterfront home. I needed to get it cleaned and fixed up. I also decided that I needed to wall off the upstairs from the downstairs once again. I figured that if it was going to be a vacation rental, there was no need for guests to have access to the basement. This should limit the number of guests and prevent large groups from booking the place.

I mentioned my need to build a wall to one of my roommates. He gladly offered to help me build it. He said he had experience in framing and construction from a summer job.

Great, I thought! I will get him to build the wall. I bought all the equipment and supplies he needed. He built the wall in one weekend and added a door with a lock so that only I could access the basement to clean it. I was so appreciative. I gave him a few hundred bucks as a thank you.

The basement had a laundry room in it, so I would use that to wash bedding, towels, etc. for turnovers.

I told my family about my new plan to list it as a vacation rental. They once again poo-poo'd the idea. Who on earth would want to pay to stay in that out-of-the-way little town? I replied, "I have nothing to lose for trying." I went ahead and listed it.

I opened a credit account at a local big-box furniture store that allowed me to defer my purchase for two years. Deferrals are another way of using other people's money. Just be sure to pay the deferral off before it comes due, or all the interest gets added to your statement.

I purchased furniture and furnishings, and a lockbox to store the house key. This way guests could check themselves in and I wouldn't have to drive twenty minutes just to meet them.

I took great photos, edited them to look even better, and did a wonderful writeup. I spent hours creating a digital guidebook to detail all there was to do within a forty-five minute drive of the property, and then I posted my listing.

I had my first booking in less than a week. And then a second and then a third. This was amazing. People were so happy to have a beautiful waterfront home. It didn't even matter that it was February and the peak of winter. My place was getting booked.

After a month or so of constant bookings, I realized that there was way more money to be made with vacation rentals than there was doing full-time rentals. There was no stress, no damage, and happy guests. I knew that I was going to keep doing this with the property. How could I not?

I started seeing someone new toward the end of March. It soon became apparent that having roommates wasn't very conducive to starting a new relationship. We lacked privacy and living with a bunch of college kids was a bit of an embarrassment factor.

Driving back and forth to do cleanings and turnovers eventually got to me. I realized that I was wasting a lot of time and it was affecting my social and personal life. I decided to move back to the waterfront home and run the vacation rental while living in the basement. I was house hacking once again, but this time I wasn't going to have roommates.

I mentioned to the guys that, when the semester was done, I didn't intend on having roommates any longer and that I was going to move back to my waterfront home. They understood and agreed to move out at the end of April.

My new relationship with Brigitte was working out incredibly well. We became very close in a short amount of time. She was a very attractive girl with a spunky personality. She was fifteen years younger than me, but we never saw the age gap. We got along amazingly well. She was very intelligent and, like a sponge, open to learning as much as she could from what I do in real estate. She was recently separated and had two little kids, a daughter, age four, and a son, age three. She was very eager to help me out when I had turnovers. We would all go to my waterfront property where the kids would have a blast running around, fishing, swimming, etc. I would pass time entertaining the kids in the yard and Brigitte insisted on handling the turnovers. This became a fun getaway activity for us all. We would then relax and watch a movie in the basement.

Brigitte was such a good companion and support. We saw eye to eye on personal and professional goals. She saw what I had accomplished in real estate in such a short amount of time and completely supported it.

When the guys vacated the duplex, I spent a month or so painting it and getting it ready to rent. Brigitte, of course, helped with a lot of it. I was truly grateful to have her and the kids in my life. What a change from every other relationship I had experienced. I knew that this relationship was different, and destiny was at play. I was an empty nester content to jump right back into the family life and take on the father role once again. The kids very quickly asked if they could call me dad. My heart melted and I had no objection. Life was taking on a new course.

Key Reader Takeaways

There are quite a few lessons in this chapter. First, you need to be open and adaptable. Changes will come and not all of them will be positive. You need to find a way to handle the situations with the best possible outcome. Having roommates is not ideal or feasible for everyone. It was, however, the right thing at the right time for me. If you are newly starting out and longing to purchase your first home, don't discount the idea of having roommates to offset your mortgage expenses. More young people should be open to this idea in order to get ahead. It may not be ideal, but it will also not be forever.

Know when to defer. I don't just mean financially, though there are great benefits in using deferred credit to purchase things you need to get ahead in your real estate investment journey. Just make sure you always pay off any deferred loan before it comes due. When you use deferred credit, if you do not pay it off when it is due, the interest charges are backdated to the date of purchase. These are often 28 percent and higher. Never pay this interest!

Refer to the professionals when needed. The big one here was when I had the tenant issues. This saved me a ton of work and stress. I devoted my attention to my properties and my new relationship. It was worth it for me to hire an expert in landlord–tenant law to handle and deal with the situation with the bad tenant. I am sure I could have handled it on my own, but there is value in offloading items to someone else so you can focus on the tasks that are more important. It may have cost more money to hire a professional, but that expenditure is also a tax write-off, so why put more on your own plate than is necessary? Let the pros do what they do.

Until now, I had lived in all my properties, multiple times. You don't have to live in your properties as I did, however, I would say this: Do not buy a property that you are not willing to live in. If you can envision yourself living there, then it can be a great home for whoever you rent it to. Additionally, if everything goes to hell in a handbasket and you needed to liquidate your properties, it is possible that it would make good financial sense for you to live in one of your rental properties. Be open to that possibility.

Be prepared for bad tenants. It will happen. I always say to people who consider becoming a landlord that having a bad tenant is a matter of when, not if. You can do all the background checks you want but, ultimately, you never know who you will be renting to. The best thing you can do to prepare is to have money set aside. I suggest at least $10,000 per property. Of course, you may not have this right away, but work toward putting money away to handle unexpected expenses or tenant/rent issues. You could also have a good line of credit to fall back on, but this will only give you more stress until you are able to pay it off.

Be open to the possibilities that come your way. I never thought I would find a relationship that complemented me on so many levels. I also didn't think that I was going to start life all over again as a dad. My life has improved immeasurably since Brigitte and the kids came along. Having the right supportive partner will truly help you in your real estate investment journey.

There will be ups and downs, but you need to stay the course.

Life was certainly changing for me. Up until now, I had done all of this on my own. Every decision I made was done without the support of someone close in my life.

My family continued to think I was crazy for spending so much time, money, and energy. At the first sign of a bad tenant, they tried to make me believe it was time to sell everything and cut my losses. Brigitte saw and shared my vision and encouraged me through my journey.

CHAPTER 8

A NEW CHAPTER

I could not believe how successful the vacation rental was. I was making nearly three times the income than I was renting it full time, and without all the hassle and heartache that tenants put me through. Not only that, but I was also doing this with the support of my new partner. Brigitte was helping in any way she could. I was truly appreciative and in debt to her.

My real estate investing was now diversified. I had accumulated several properties by this point. I had maximized earnings from them by creating secondary suites where possible. I had successfully entered the world of vacation rentals. I was finally making a really good income that exceeded that of my professor salary. And I had the support of a wonderful woman and her two kids who enhanced my life in ways I never expected.

Brigitte continued to help me out when I had guest turnover at the waterfront home. I would keep the kids entertained in the yard and along the waterfront. She would take care of the turnover without expecting anything in return. That's right, she wouldn't take any financial compensation for her work. She felt that it was what one does to show their love and support for the other person. We grew very close.

As a recently separated woman with two kids, Brigitte was living with her parents. She happened to mention that she wanted to get out on her own. She hated the fact that she was an adult forced to live at home. She wanted a secure place to raise her kids and be proud to call home. The problem was, she didn't have much income as a stay-at-home mother.

I always considered myself a problem solver. I felt bad that she was caught in limbo. I knew that she wouldn't be able to afford a decent home, and what she could afford would likely not be in a good area. I weighed the pros and cons and then sat her down and said, "You know, the duplex that you helped me paint and clean is move-in ready. I still haven't found a tenant I am comfortable renting to."

Brigitte was surprised and said that she couldn't afford the rent I was asking for that place. I told her that, since I had experienced what a really bad tenant is like, I was worried about getting stuck in the same situation. She would actually be helping me out and doing me a favor by living there. I offered her the place at half the cost of what fair-market value rent was plus the cost of utilities. She was incredibly appreciative of the offer, but declined. She wanted to do things on her own and not be the recipient of a handout. I told her that it wasn't a handout. I could get first and last month's rent from a new tenant and that could be all I see from them. They could leave me with all kinds of damage, and it could take months and months to evict them. Ultimately, I could end up losing more money by holding out for top dollar than by offering the place to her for half price.

She asked, "What if we break up?" I said that, even if that were to happen, knowing what type of person she was, I wouldn't regret having her live there. I reminded her that, when my last relationship ended, I was the one who moved out of the house into a one-bedroom apartment rather than displacing my ex and her three kids. I said that they are still renting that place from me and there are no issues.

She gave it some thought, looked me deep in my eyes, and said, "Okay, as long as you are really sure, I will live in your duplex."

I was happy to know that I could help Brigitte and her kids and have someone good who would be taking care of the place. Brigitte decided she would move into the place right away, except there was one problem . . . she had no furniture. I said, "No problem, let's go to the same furniture store that I had purchased all the furnishings for my Airbnb property." Now she really gave me that look.

"Are you kidding?" she proclaimed. "I can't pay half price for a rental and allow you to buy me the furniture to furnish it with, no way!"

I assured her once again that it was okay. I said I wouldn't be buying anything for her. We could put her furniture on my store credit and defer the payments by 15 months. She would be buying it, but I would be using my credit to allow her to get it up front.

Brigitte sat silent for some time and finally looked up and said no matter what, she was going to pay back the loan as soon as she could. I told her not to sweat it. It was deferred for fifteen months with no payments and no interest. She said she understood but was still adamant that she was going to pay it off in a matter of months.

We drove to the furniture store and she picked out all that she needed and didn't go overboard. She made very careful purchases. Buying nice but cheaper items, looking in the as-is room for clearance items, and even negotiating with the manager to give her a better deal on some things. Oh, man. A girl after my own heart. She was frugal and didn't mind asking for a deal. This girl really appealed to my Dutch sensibilities.

The furniture was delivered in a couple of days and Brigitte and the kids moved in. She immediately began to take the place over and make it her own. It was her place to raise her kids and she felt like she was gaining independence.

I was all too happy to help her out as she continued to help me out. I had frequent guest turnovers at my Airbnb and she continued to handle those turnovers all by herself. The four of us were inseparable and we grew closer and closer to each other.

I still maintained my residence in the lower level of the waterfront home, but let's be honest, Brigitte and I were never really apart. We spent so much time at each other's places. The independence she longed for was actually an interdependence. We needed each other and we were never apart. How great life continued to be for us. The Airbnb property was flourishing.

True to her word, Brigitte handed me the cash in full within six months of us putting her furniture on my deferred credit. I was blown away! She didn't have to do that. She could have used the full fifteen months to pay it off and not put herself so tight. I knew that this girl was different, and I had so much respect for her.

Being the ever-creative strategist, I told her I was not going to pay off my deferred credit right now but that her obligation to it was done. I loved the idea of interest-free money. I would have no problem paying that debt off before it came due. So, I put the money to use where I needed it immediately. Renovations. More on that in the next chapter.

Key Reader Takeaways

Diversifying your income is not only a really good idea, but also essential to beginning your real estate investing career with that goal in mind. You should always look at what potential a property has. Can it be split into separate units? Can you run a good short-term vacation rental for even greater income, flexibility, and freedom? Of course, you need to consult your local by-laws and requirements before embarking on any of these courses of action.

Once you diversify, you not only maximize profit, but you also minimize losses. If you have a single property that is one unit and a tenant either leaves or stops paying rent, you have just lost 100 percent of your rental income. When you maximize the potential by adding a unit and/or purchasing other multi-unit properties, you're no longer in danger of losing all your rental income. Two properties with two units results in the loss of 25 percent of your income if a tenant leaves. As soon as you can, leverage your first property to buy more. You will sleep better at night knowing that you can float things if something goes awry.

I can't stress enough how important it is to have a partner who supports you. You need to have someone who shares the vision and will do whatever they can to build you up, and you should do the same for them in return. What I did for Brigitte was a calculated risk. It really could have bitten me in the ass, big time! If the relationship had turned, I could have been stuck with a tenant paying half price and left with the furniture bill. Luckily, this was not the case.

This ended up being a short chapter, but it has remained one of the longest and best chapters of my life. Brigitte and I remain strong today, and we continue to support each other in our individual goals, dreams, and desires. This real estate investment journey is best started when you are single and can make decisions on your own without having to worry about how it will impact other people in your life. Having said that, it is compounded in so many ways when you have the right person in your life who will be a support rather than a naysayer.

Be open to possibilities!

CHAPTER 9
HOUSE HACK ATTACK!

A good tenant is more than just someone who pays the rent on time. Sometimes a tenant can be considered a nuisance when they have unreasonable demands. If they don't listen to reason, then it may be time for a drastic change.

Eventually, I was getting some flak from the lower tenant in the house where my ex was renting. He started getting really demanding. He devised a list of must-have items. I looked this list over and thought, what the hell? If I did all of this, it would cost over $10,000! There was no way I was about to do that. Sure, he pays his rent on time, but meeting his demands was ludicrous and unnecessary.

Being a landlord is not all peaches and cream. Tenants can cause stress in compounding ways. The lower-level tenant's $10,000 list of demands finally took its toll. There was no way I needed to do all those things, and there was no way I was going to spend that kind of money just to appease him. I was losing sleep and the wheels began to turn.

I think my true turning point for this nuisance tenant was when he told me he was going to be about a week late paying his rent. Not only was he making unreasonable demands, but now he wanted me to be understanding of his circumstances. In and of itself, I prefer communication when a tenant is going to be late. A one-time late payment really doesn't bother me. It was the fact that this tenant was really annoying me. I knew something drastic needed to happen.

When Brigitte got home, I sat her down to have a discussion. I talked about how I was getting really stressed and annoyed by the problem tenant. She already knew the situation, as we talked about everything together. What she didn't know was that he was late on his rent or that I was losing sleep again. I was really worried that I might be heading for a repeat of the horrible tenants I had at my waterfront property earlier that year.

She replied, "Kick him out!" I said that I would love to, but that, legally, I can only get rid of a tenant if I go "owner occupied," meaning I had to take over the unit myself. I said that I could do that, but I really didn't want to leave the lower level of the waterfront property vacant. It wasn't suitable to be another Airbnb listing, as the noise between the floors was too great. Guests would complain and I would get terrible reviews.

I told her that I was going to move out of the waterfront home and tear down the wall that separated the upstairs and downstairs. I was tired of making the forty-minute round trip for turnovers. It really ate up our weekends, as we couldn't go anywhere or do much of anything. I was making great money from Airbnb, but the work involved was getting to me. Brigitte was also getting tired of cleaning that place.

I drafted an eviction notice, citing owner occupation, and delivered it to the annoying/delinquent tenant in the basement. He took the notice and said, "Fine!"

I was shocked that he left right away. There was no waiting. It happened in less than twenty-four hours. This was unheard of. Now things could really proceed.

I moved my stuff from the waterfront property to the basement suite where my ex was living upstairs. I actually loved being in that space and was excited to share it with Brigitte and the kids when they came over . . . which really was all the time. When I wasn't spending time at their place, they were spending time at mine. We had really gelled and just couldn't stay away from each other. And really, why should we?

We all enjoyed the basement suite. It was actually very cool. We loved the space. It was perfect for us. The rec room was massive, and we made use of the hot rock sauna every night after the kids were in bed. It was our getaway from the world. We would bring our beverages in and bake ourselves for forty-five minutes to an hour. We would enjoy each other's company, share ideas, plan our future, and just unwind. It was very comfortable there. The kids were happy and we were enjoying it, too.

Life was great. The kids really felt at home in the new basement suite, and we absolutely loved our one-on-one time in the sauna each night. I really thought life was perfect and I was content to share time at each other's places. That is, until I started looking at local listings.

I often checked the realtor's website listings as well as the website for community listings. One day, I happened to look under the short-term accommodations section and noticed that some hydro workers were in need of a place for several months. I contacted them and offered them my waterfront home. They were not looking to spend that much on rent and really didn't want to stay in the next town over, so I told them I might have another solution and would email them again later that night.

As soon as Brigitte got home, I told her that we needed to talk. I said, "Hear me out before you get upset and kill the idea." She knew right away that I'd come up with a doozy of another creative, hair-brained idea. She also knew that my ideas always had the best outcomes and resulted in me getting ahead financially. She took a deep breath, sat back, and waited to hear what I was going to say.

I also took a deep breath, followed by a hard swallow, and said, "You know, my basement suite is over 2,200 square feet... It has two bedrooms that the kids are already used to . . . What if you and the kids moved in for a little while?"

She replied, "Okay . . ." but kept looking at me, in complete silence, knowing there was more to my crazy idea.

The silence was deafening. I'm pretty sure that, by the time I finished that sentence, my eyes were squeezed tight shut. I left them shut like that for a few moments. I opened one eye and then the other to see Brigitte giving me that look . . . Uh oh . . . I was in trouble! Then she replied, "Why? Have you found someone to rent my place at market rent?"

I was stunned. How did she know? She was very perceptive and smart. "Actually . . . yes," I replied. I told her how I found these four out-of-town hydro workers who needed a place for five or six months. They needed it fully furnished and they were able to pay above market rent. I told her that I had offered them the Airbnb on the water, but they declined it. I told them I would get back to them with another option.

She let out a deep sigh, threw her hands in the air, and asked when they needed it. I told her that they needed it in a few days. She really wasn't happy. She loved her independence and the home she had made in the duplex, but she also knew I was stressed and needed a complicated, multi-part solution to achieve the best possible outcome.

She agreed to my insane idea and, within 48 hours, she moved most of her belongings from the five-bedroom duplex into my two-bedroom basement suite that was already full of my own furniture. Lucky for us, the space was so big that we found a way to accommodate most of it, and the items that didn't fit, we squeezed into a storage room. It was filled from wall to wall and from floor to ceiling. It was crazy, but it allowed everything to work out.

Back to the waterfront house. The Airbnb bookings slowed down due to the changing seasons. I needed to find tenants to rent it. A three-generation family came forward. I thought it was great! They were on government assistance but, collectively, they could afford what I was asking for the place. Of course, they wanted the entire house as they needed all five bedrooms. So, I agreed to remove the wall and rented the entire space. I would later come to realize why this can be problematic. More on this in a later chapter.

Life was great once again. We were enjoying our new space. The hydro workers moved into the duplex, so I was earning double what Brigitte was paying. I rented the waterfront home to full-time tenants. All was right in my real estate ventures.

Back to where we were living. We did enjoy life there, but there will always be an issue when you bring together two worlds that collide. If you recall, the upper unit belonged to my ex-girlfriend, her new boyfriend, and her three kids. Not that there were any overt issues. We were all adults and I had hoped that we would get along fine; however, soon came some passive-aggressiveness from her boyfriend. The driveway was very long and, to allow us to pull up to the carport next to the house and access the double garage, they needed to park on the right side of the driveway. More often than not, this didn't happen. Parking was done haphazardly and, in some cases, he would crank his wheels out all the way to the left, which made it even more of an obstacle to squeeze by.

That was one element that started getting on our nerves. The other was that they were beginning to make excess noise that came through the floor. It really seemed deliberate, especially after the kids were tucked into bed, like they knew the noise would wake them. Now we couldn't enjoy our relaxing escape in the sauna because the kids were awake and upset.

To add to that, the odd comment was hurled Brigitte's way when she came home. She was definitely made to feel uncomfortable and unwelcome. This was her home, but it was beginning not to feel that way. Something needed to be done.

Despite repeated requests to deal with the issues, nothing seemed to change. Brigitte was getting to her wit's end and I was very frustrated. It didn't need to be like this. But, it also didn't have to be like this.

I am prone to make snap decisions. So, I drafted the legally required document and gave it to my ex. They had sixty days to vacate the property, as I was going owner occupied. My ex was not happy and tried to give me a piece of her mind. I wasn't having any of it and wasn't about to get into a dialogue. I turned and walked away while she was still talking.

That set the tone. We knew it was likely going to get worse before it got better. We were prepared to wait out the sixty days to freedom.

The days seemed to drag on. The passive-aggressive antics continued to rise. Brigitte wasn't happy and I kept encouraging her to just wait it out. It was not easy. It was a long, long two months.

Finally, the day came when the moving truck showed up. They were leaving and we couldn't be happier. At the end of a long day of them loading their truck, my ex knocked on my door to hand me the keys. As I took them, she said, "You know, I am not happy about how all this turned—" I didn't let her finish. I closed the door, turned, and walked away. I didn't care what she had to say. It was over. I wanted her to move on with her life as I moved on with mine.

Brigitte and the kids were really excited to see the upstairs. As soon as we had the keys, we went straight in. The kids claimed their bedrooms and ran around, completely happy with the new space. Our son turned to me and asked about the downstairs. I said we were going to have that, too. We just needed to get rid of the wall separating the two units. So, I kicked the wall in front of us. His eyes lit up and he let out a warrior cry and started kicking, too. We all started laughing.

Soon enough, we broke through to the other side. He was still in his ninja warrior mode and let out another cry as he attacked a different wall. We said, "No, buddy! Not that wall, just this one!" It was too cute. His little four-year-old body couldn't do that much damage, and it really set the tone of fun and excitement in our new space.

We settled in quickly. We were all happy and, for a time, content.

The sauna became therapy for us. Not just for the benefits of physical well-being, but also for mental therapy. We would just sit in there and listen to each other. We encouraged each other and it became a safe place for us to open up. Sometimes I would pour my heart and soul out to Brigitte, look for the wisdom she had to offer. Other times, Brigitte looked to me for guidance. I recall one such discussion where she was feeling uneasy. This feeling wasn't born out of insecurity, nor was it about the financial burdens I was incurring with all the debt from properties and maxing out my deferrals at the big-box stores to renovate units between tenants. Her discontent was centered around the fact that she was looking at all my success and achievements and feeling like we were worlds apart. She felt like she would never be able to catch up. We kept discussing how, when the kids were old enough, we would take an early retirement, but in reality, it left her feeling like she had nothing to contribute.

Her greatest fear, after coming out of a bad marriage, was having to rely on me financially to float her wants, needs, and desires when we finally took that step to early retirement. She had been controlled before and, though there was no sign of that in our relationship, she felt that it was a cause for concern.

Our discussions in the sauna diverted us from focusing on our happy future to trying to convince her that she wasn't behind in life. She kept saying, "I have nothing going for myself financially. You are so successful, and I don't want to have to rely on you in retirement to come with my hand out saying I need my nails done."

She kept comparing herself to her peers. She said that other people her age had college degrees, travelled, and established their careers. I reminded her that she was successful. She chose a different path. She decided to get married and have children when she was twenty-two. She would be miles ahead of her peers when it came to retirement. Her peers didn't have kids yet. They would be in the thick of raising kids when we decided to take the plunge into retirement.

It made her feel a little better, but it was hard to focus on future things to satisfy current situations. Brigitte was discontent because she felt like she wasn't contributing financially to our future. She was contributing to expenses and never took a handout from me. She was very proud that way, but she still felt uneasy about having no real financial prospects to get ahead.

Brigitte was working as a realtor's assistant at this time. She loved her job and was loving the aspect of real estate balancing off what she knew and had learned from my experiences in real estate. It was perfect for her. She was learning lots and was even teaching me some things. I was incredibly proud of her.

One day, Brigitte came home incredibly excited. She just got the inside scoop from her boss about a bank-owned property. This property was in an incredible vacation area near our home. This place had a world-class beach, camping, vineyards, micro-breweries, art galleries, art studios, fine dining, boating, fishing, and more. This house was in the heart of it all.

It had six bedrooms upstairs, a large eat-in kitchen, a dining room, and a four-piece bathroom with a corner jacuzzi tub. The property also had over 300 feet of depth and 70 feet of road frontage. It was in a quiet location just off a main highway. The wonderful neighbors were all homeowners. This property seemed too good to be true. The best part was the price. It was less than what some recreational vehicles cost.

We discussed it that night in the sauna. She was on fire. She loved this property and wished that she could buy it to start her own real estate journey. She was bummed that she didn't have any money. I said, "You need to buy this house. This is too good a deal to pass up."

Brigitte replied, "But I don't have a down payment." I told her not to worry about that. "What do you mean?" she asked. I told her I would loan her the down payment because I didn't want to see her miss out." Sure, I could have moved on the property myself, but there was a greater benefit in being able to help Brigitte purchase the place for her own investment.

She began to protest and said that she was not a charity case. I told her that it wasn't charity. It was a loan. Buy the house, we will fix it up, and then put it on Airbnb.

Reluctantly, she agreed. She knew that another deal this good would never come up again. She also knew I was right and that she needed this to get into the real estate game. This was her in. It was also her way to contribute financially and feel like this part of her life was moving forward. It meant that having kids early didn't put her behind her peers after all. This deal represented her independence as well as her future.

The next day, she spoke to her boss about it and her boss was incredibly supportive. Her boss took her to look at it that day. I didn't even know she was going for a viewing. She flexed her independence, took one look at the property, knew it needed work but also realized it was a diamond in the rough. She told her boss that she wanted to make an offer. They drove back to the office and her boss called the listing agent. There were three other registered offers on the table. Brigitte was told that she had to put her best offer forward.

Brigitte didn't skip a beat. She said, "I'm not into competition. I refuse to overpay." She stuck to her guns and offered what she thought the property was worth.

Now it was a waiting game. The bank was going to take 48 hours to assess all offers and decide.

Brigitte took those two days to make an appointment with her bank. She provided the listing and a copy of the offer and asked her bank if she could get a mortgage. The bank was shocked. They said they hadn't financed a mortgage that low in many, many years. They weren't even sure the underwriter would consider such a low mortgage. After all, some cars cost more.

The next two days were nerve-racking. Our nights in the sauna were filled with discussions around our hopes that she got it and fears of her not getting it. She was so nervous and excited all at once.

The next day, she got some good news from the bank. They were pre-approving her for the mortgage she needed to buy the home. She was so excited! One major hurtle was out of the way . . . Now only twenty-four more hours to hear from the bank.

That night was filled with more excitement and trepidation while we sat in the sauna. I was excited for her, and she was anxious. She just wanted an answer.

Brigitte went to work the next day and asked her boss if she had heard anything. Her boss told her that they went with one of the other offers. Brigitte was deflated.

When we got our alone time in the sauna that night, the mood was sombre. She was upset. She once again felt like she was never going to amount to anything. She wasn't going to get ahead. I told her that other good deals will come, as they always do. She looked at me and said, "Not deals like that!" I knew she was right, but I also knew that the right deal would come at the right time.

We went on with our lives. A few weeks passed by before her boss suddenly said to her, "I guess the deal on that bank-owned property fell through. It's back on the market as of a few moments ago. Do you still want to make your offer?"

"What? Yes! But what about the other three offers?" Brigitte asked.

Her boss replied, "I guess none of them were interested enough to come back to the table. Shall I resubmit your original offer?"

Brigitte thought for a moment and told her boss to lower her original offer by $10,000. Her boss said, "Are you sure? It is already the cheapest property I have seen in years." Brigitte told her to submit the lower offer.

Her boss submitted it and followed up with a phone call directly to the agent. They talked for a bit and then she hung up. Not much later, a call came in. They accepted Brigitte's offer. She was going to be a homeowner!

She closed on the property and we immediately went to work. We assessed what the property needed right away. I used my deferred credit at the big-box store to buy new flooring, tile, and paint. We got busy right away, and when I say we, I mean me. I did all the work getting her property ready. I had the time since I was off work during the summer. The repairs were not beyond my skill level. I was quite happy to work and get the house ready for her. I just wanted to see her succeed, get ahead, and feel like she was accomplishing something. She had already supported me in ways that went above and beyond, and now it was my turn to support her.

In five or six weeks, we finished everything that needed to be done. The property looked cute and ready to be listed on Airbnb. Brigitte got a booking right away. It was a long-term booking from someone who was building a house in the area. She was so happy.

Eventually, the guest who booked the place found flaws in the property and made some complaints. It wasn't a five-star property, and we knew it. His rate was a fraction of what it would cost to book any other property in the region. This didn't stop him from complaining. That started weighing on Brigitte. The last straw for her was when he checked out and left a bad review. Her first review and it was a bad one. She felt like she couldn't recover from that rating.

She removed the property from Airbnb and listed it as a full-time rental. Her first tenants gave her a sob story and she took pity on them. They were women, and Brigitte understood their situation and wanted to cut them a break. She rented it to them.

It wasn't long before she realized she'd made a mistake. They were late with the rent and were causing issues. They ended up leaving a short while into the lease.

She found new tenants and they turned out to be professionals. That is, tenants who know how to work the system. Brigitte got no money from them and it took several months to get a hearing. They played every trick in the book. They got a stay for the eviction order, which prolonged the nonpayment, stress, and anxiety a little longer. Luckily, she got the house so cheap that it really didn't cost much to carry. But still, she felt horrible, angry, and let down by the landlord and tenant laws.

Eventually, she got her eviction order, but it could only be served by the sheriff. That took another month or so. The professional tenants waited till the last minute to leave. They actually waited for the sheriff to evict them and change the locks. But at least they were out and, thankfully, other than garbage and furniture being left behind, there was no damage.

This experience was enough for Brigitte. She didn't have the stomach for it, and she felt she was a poor judge of character and was completely turned off by real estate investment.

She listed the house privately and sold it to a couple. She made way, way, way, way more than she originally paid and invested in it. She did very well on this deal. She may not have been an ongoing real estate investor, but as a prolonged flipper (two years) she did amazingly well. I was still proud of her for trying and I was super proud of her for what she walked away with after selling the house in such a short amount of time.

Key Reader Takeaways

Being flexible and adaptable allowed me to handle a few complicated situations, with multi-part solutions, in a short amount of time. The end result was always improving quality of life as well as financial gain.

Brigitte followed my lead, trusting me blindly, even though it made her uncomfortable and meant making a rapid change. You cannot dictate this kind of situation to your partner and expect that they will go along with it. The decision needs to be a mutual one.

We made the best of the situation and grew close in several ways by having that "us time" in the sauna each night. We spoke about our hopes and dreams for ourselves and the kids, and about our lives and future real estate investing. I wasn't done with my real estate journey and Brigitte was along for a ride that was just taking off. It kept us on the same page and really helped to bounce ideas off one another.

It is also important to involve your children (if you have any) or partner in some of the fun of demolition and sprucing a place up. It can be a great bonding experience and it really gives everyone a sense of pride and ownership.

Support needs to go both ways. You need to support your partner's dreams and aspirations if you expect them to support yours. I could easily have purchased the house that Brigitte bought for myself, but there was so much opportunity for her to learn and grow. I was happy to invest the time and money to help her and she was equally happy to pay me back upon the sale of the home. She learned a lot from that process, and one of those things was that what I did was not something she needed or wanted to do. It was enough to have one real estate investor in the house, we didn't need to both be in the game.

The other lesson is that you will run into trouble as a landlord. I always tell people that it is not if but rather when. You need to have an iron stomach to get into this business. You will run into situations that cause you stress and anxiety, and cause you to lose sleep. Try to remain calm. It is a business. Do not take things personally. Be prepared and have some money put away for each rental. Having a kitty saved up will allow you to weather a storm of bad tenants, make a major repair, or have a vacant unit. Don't spend all the money you get from rent. Save a portion and plan ahead.

You can succeed in this business!

Being a landlord is not always easy. Having said that, being a landlord can be very rewarding. Once you get the bug, you will want to keep going.

CHAPTER 10

THE MANSION

Our evening routine of enjoying a glass of wine (or three) in the sauna and talking about the future definitely left me wanting to pursue more opportunities in real estate.

I continued to go to the bar to get inspired by my two landlord friends. Whenever I spoke to the one with 200 units, he encouraged me to keep going. He spoke about his assistant who bought his first home, and then a second, and then quickly kept adding to his portfolio. Before long, this guy quit his full-time job to live off his rental business. His job was holding him back from opportunity.

I told my friend what the bank told me a few years ago. They said I had to cool it down after buying three properties and that I likely wouldn't get approved for another mortgage for the next few years. My friend said that I could use private financing.

Private financing? What's that? My friend (who talked like Tony Soprano and even looked like him: large stature, gold chains around his neck and wrist) said, "It is when you go to a guy in Toronto and he finances it and you pay him points."

Wow, I thought. That sounded a little sketchy to me. Would I be going to the mob for a loan? It scared me and I really didn't think any more about it. I decided that I liked my kneecaps where they were. I just simply thought, well . . . the bank told me to cool it for a few years. It has now been a few years, maybe I could get approved again?

I began looking on the real estate listing website for more investment opportunities. I kept hearing my land-lord friends go on about opportunities in commercial real estate. I decided to change my search parameters and switched the filter from residential to commercial. That was quite interesting to view. I did come across a very exciting listing. It was a building on the main street in a town forty minutes from where I lived. This was quite rural, the perfect definition of "small town." What was intriguing about the listing was that, not only was it a commercial building with commercial space on the lower level, it also included the active business that was running there. It was a laundromat. How cool, I thought. As I kept reading the listing, I noted that it had five rented apartments above. The best part was that it was asking well under what it would cost to set up the infrastructure for the laundromat alone. I had to check this one out.

I made an appointment and toured the space with Brigitte's realtor boss. I met the tenants, who seemed decent, and the apartments were in good condition. The laundromat was only operating at half capacity. Quite a few machines were out of order. Even still, I thought this was a great source of alternative cash income. I would totally be willing to drive the 80-minute round trip once a week to check on the laundromat and empty the machines' coins. I could even look into expanding that business to take on dry cleaning and maybe hire someone to do wash-and-fold services.

I was so excited to get into the commercial market so inexpensively. How could I not move on this opportunity? I made an offer right away and it was accepted. I then called my mortgage broker and said that I wanted to buy a commercial building. I sent her a copy of the listing and made an appointment to discuss financing.

When I got to her office, she was beaming. She couldn't believe that I was about to go at it again. I could see how proud she was of how far I had come in such a short time. She was going to pull out all the stops to make this happen.

What I didn't realize about commercial property was that certain requirements are different for them than they are for residential properties. I was told that I would need a Phase 1 Environmental Site Assessment and possibly a Phase 2 ESA for the lender. This could cost several thousand dollars for each study. The other difficult news she gave me was that I would need at least a 35 percent down payment. She also told me that commercial property didn't fall under her portfolio, as she could only finance up to a fourplex. Purchases beyond a fourplex required the commercial lending department, but she told me to leave it with her and she would see what could be done. She then paused and said, "You know, if I can't get funding here at the bank, I got a guy who may be able to hook you up."

I said, "You got a guy?"

She replied, "I got a guy!"

I left feeling a little deflated. This was such an incredibly good deal. I couldn't pass it up. I was worried about what the bank would say, and I was curious about this guy whom my mortgage broker had lined up to help me if she couldn't.

A few days went by before I got a call from my mortgage broker. She said, "Well Rob, I discussed it at length with our commercial lender, we went over all the numbers, we looked at your portfolio, and determined that you should be able to pull off buying this property." I wasn't surprised, but I was still ecstatic. I had crunched the numbers, too. I knew how much money the place was pulling in. I also knew how much money I was making from my rental properties plus my professor salary. Of course I could pull this off.

She then went on to say, "But . . . there's an issue . . ."

Issue? What issue? If the numbers look good, how could there be an issue? She said, "We tried both major under-

writers and they each came back saying the same thing...
They will not finance a rural, commercial property."

What? Why? How? "Can they do that? It sounds like discrimination against small communities to me," I replied.

"Well, yeah, they can do whatever they want. They are the lender," she said.

"That isn't fair. How do other people buy commercial properties in small towns?" I asked.

She said, "I guess they either use cash, or leverage their properties or lines of credit, or they bought before the bank was shy on lending to rural commercial."

Damn it! I was so close. How could I let this incredible deal slip between my fingers? I then asked my broker, "What about the guy you said you had?"

She said excitedly, "I do got a guy!" She hooked me up with a local broker. She said he specialized in A, B, and private lenders (A lenders are big banks. B Lenders are non-banks and credit unions).

Great! Maybe this deal wasn't dead yet. I called him up and made an appointment. Unfortunately, his lenders said the same thing. They were unwilling to finance rural commercial properties. He also said that, for the same reason, he didn't have any private lenders who were willing to finance it. They were worried that, if I defaulted, they would be stuck with a property that they couldn't sell to recoup their investment.

That's it. The deal was dead. I called my agent, who then relayed the info to the sellers. The sellers then retorted that they would be willing to hold the mortgage for me. I would just have to pay them the 35 percent down payment and they would hold the balance of the mortgage as a vender take-back loan at 7 percent.

I was blown away. This deal could still work. I could make my entry into the commercial market and become a business owner all in one. I discussed the opportunity at length with Brigitte. We thought about how great it would be to own a small apartment building and a commercial laundromat. We talked at length about the great opportunities the laundromat could present and how we could expand that business. I told her that I was very excited but needed to sleep on it before making a decision.

I don't think I slept much that night. I was racking my brain as to what to do. I woke up the next morning still unsure of my decision. Finally, after weighing all the pros and cons, I made up my mind.

I called my realtor and said, "Please tell the lenders that I was completely blown away by their offer to hold the mortgage on the property. Tell them thank you, but I have decided not to go through with the purchase. Please send over the release forms."

She was stunned. "Why are you not going through with the purchase? They're willing to finance it."

I replied, "I know, I think it's amazing, but ultimately, there's a reason no lender wants to finance this property. If I decided to sell it in a couple of years, I could be in the same boat they are. I would be stuck with an unsellable property. Tell them it's too great a risk for me and I am going to have to withdraw my offer."

My real estate agent understood. She prepared the documents and, with that, the deal was dead.

In retrospect, I really should have taken the owners of the laundromat up on the offer for the VTB. I should have gone through with the purchase. It was a good deal and real estate really started to rise in value a few years later. That was hindsight being 20/20; however, if I had done that deal, I wouldn't have been able to do what I did next.

Everything happens for a reason. Because that deal died, I went back to looking at opportunities on the residential listings. Unfortunately, I couldn't find anything in the price range of the laundromat. I had limited funds and couldn't afford an expensive property. After that thought left my head, I was curious about what I would find if I increased my search parameters to include something much more expensive.

Oh, boy! What I found blew me away. There was this stunning 6,700 square-foot Victorian mansion for sale . . . one of the biggest in our city. It had a double-sized living room, a gorgeous dining room, a massive eat-in kitchen, two marble fireplaces, seven incredibly large bedrooms, five bathrooms, five additional fireplaces, a gorgeous wooden staircase, a servants' staircase at the back, two separate wings, a second living room upstairs, a finished basement with a games room and pool table, a laundry room, a couple of storage rooms, a separate entry, an over-sized garage with a coach house apartment above it, nine-foot doors, an enclosed porch, decks running around half of the house, a gorgeous yard with incredible gardens, a courtyard, and an in-ground swimming pool.

I couldn't believe how beautiful this place was. I immediately looked at it as an investment. I could buy this gorgeous home and close off the north wing to keep it separate from the rest of the house. The north wing had its own entry off the driveway. It had a gas fireplace on the lower level and a gorgeous three-piece bathroom on the lower level. It had its own staircase that led to the upper level where there were two bedrooms, a private living room, and a large four-piece bathroom with a jacuzzi tub.

The coach house was a separate unit I could make income from, and the basement had potential to be turned into a separate two-bedroom apartment. Best of all, we could move into the main part of the mansion and upgrade our standard of living. Now this was looking like an amazing opportunity. The only problem was . . . I had to convince Brigitte that this would be a good move.

When we were in the sauna that night, I said, "You know, I was looking at the realtor's website and I think

I found another amazing investment property." She was intrigued. I told her all about this house and how we could rent two units on Airbnb and make a two-bedroom apartment in the basement.

She said, "What about the main part of the house? And can you really afford such a large and nice place?"

I took a deep breath and then swallowed hard. "Hear me out before you get upset or shoot the idea down."

I could see it in her eyes. She was thinking, here we go again!

I said, "What if we move into the mansion? It would up our standard of living and I could easily find a tenant to rent the house we're currently in."

Again, it seemed like an eternity of silence. I kept looking at her and she kept staring at me. Then she replied, "All right, book an appointment to view it. I'll look at it, but I am not making any commitments or promises."

That was good enough for me. I called Brigitte's boss and asked her to arrange a viewing of the mansion. Within a day, we were touring the inside of this gorgeous home. It was so big, with so much to see, that it took over an hour for us just to walk through and look around. At one point, Brigitte and I got separated and we bumped into each other again in the massive living room. She didn't say a word . . . she just looked at me.

I said, "Well, what do you think?"

She said, "You know, I agreed to the viewing because I thought it would appease you, and then I wanted to tell you how it wouldn't work well for us because I love our current home so much, but I have to say . . . I am falling in love with this place!"

"Really?" I said. "So, you would be willing to move here?"

She said "Yes, but on one condition—You cannot sell our current house. If things don't seem great here after we move in, I am moving back to the other home. You can stay in the mansion alone."

We called her boss over and told her to write up an offer. I really lowballed the offer. Even though the place was gorgeous inside, it had been neglected outside. It was so overgrown with trees that you couldn't see the house from the road. It had nineties decor in the kitchen and other items of wear would be highlighted in the offer. The house had been on the market for over 180 days. I found out that it was a divorce situation. Neither owner wanted to hang onto this gorgeous gem. I think, for most people, it would be too much house for one person, but I wasn't looking to have all that space for myself. I was looking to make an income from it and enjoy living there at the same time.

The offer was submitted and then rejected and signed back. We countersigned, the owner countered again, and then, finally, we accepted.

The offer was written to include must-have items for insurance: No knob and tube wiring; removal of any asbestos; and leave all the furniture. I wanted to make this as easy as possible for her to accept. She was divorced and no longer living there. She didn't need the hassle and stress of moving, selling, or storing the contents of the home. I knew I was stretching myself thin to make this deal. I needed that furniture to fill the massive home and to get the Airbnb up and running right away. She accepted all those terms.

The house closed and we were excited to move in. When we got there on moving day, the seller met us and explained that she had issues with the remediation crew and fired them. She was looking for a new crew to finish the removal of the asbestos.

We were not happy. This left the basement out of bounds. It was taped up in plastic. We couldn't fully move in and enjoy the entire space. We had to pile a bunch of furniture up in the dining room on the main level, which meant we couldn't make use of the upstairs either.

It impacted our enjoyment of the new home and left us concerned about whether we would be exposed to asbestos. Finally, three weeks later, they were done. We were able to move in fully, but we were still apprehensive. What if fibers were still floating around in the basement? We decided to wait a few more weeks before using the basement or moving furniture down there.

I sued the seller for not meeting the conditions of the sale. On the advice of my lawyer, they said to let her facilitate and pay for the rest of the remediation, as we shouldn't take any action until that was complete. The previous owner was shocked when she was served a letter of intent. She wasn't going to pay our demand until she was advised that we were within our rights and being very reasonable. She agreed to settle without having to take any further action. So, I got an even better deal on the mansion than what the sale agreement stated.

Once we moved in, we shuffled furniture around in the north wing and the coach house. Priority #1 was not to move in and enjoy. It was to get our listings live on Airbnb and begin making an income to pay for the costs of the mansion.

We got a booking within one week of listing, and then another, and another. Holy cow! This thing was going to work. It is so satisfying seeing a leap of faith come to fruition in the way you had hoped. Actually, beyond what I had hoped!

The mansion was massive. Way bigger than anything we had been in before. We didn't even notice or miss the space being rented on Airbnb. In fact, our living space was still incredibly immense. We weren't even using all of *that* space.

We decided to maximize even more income potential. We called a contractor and had him make a few modifications to the basement to turn it into a fully separate two-bedroom apartment. We installed a kitchen and put up a wall to create a second bedroom. A week after the renovation was complete, we rented that apartment to an acquaintance and her two kids.

The mansion was making money hand over fist, and we were loving our enhanced lifestyle. It turned out to be an amazing investment—Even better than the commercial building I had walked away from.

We were very happy there.

You will upgrade your life, too!

KEY READER TAKEAWAYS

I've said it before, and I will say it again. It is extremely important to be creative. Creative to find solutions. Creative to secure financing. Creative to maximize profits and creative to make your investments attractive to tenants and guests.

Along with creativity, add focus, resiliency, and determination. These characteristics will help you as you begin or continue your real estate investment journey.

Another thing to keep in mind is that not every deal will work out. Sometimes it's best to walk away. In hindsight, it would have been a great investment if I had moved on the commercial building with five apartments and the laundromat. Having said that, and not having a crystal ball, maybe those tenants were an issue. Maybe the building had underlying issues. Maybe the laundromat wouldn't have been successful. Despite all of that, there would have been a tremendous growth in equity, as property values skyrocketed a few years later.

Despite the building's potential, if I had gone through with the deal, I would have been stretched so thin at the time that I wouldn't have been able to move on another property for a little while. I certainly would not have increased my search parameters to include values that I didn't think I would get approved for. Had the commercial building gone through, I would not have ended up in the mansion. Not only was the mansion an amazing place to live, but it ended up garnering way more income than the commercial building would have, and it was appreciating at a far greater rate.

Do not regret your decisions. You will make decisions based on what's right for you at that time. The future you may have a different opinion and you can't deal with future you today.

Weigh your options and decide what is right for you in the moment. Don't let fear hold you back. Fear is not a reason. Fear is a detractor from your financial goals and success. If fear isn't holding you back, maybe it's something more pragmatic. Often, it's the banks. Banks are awful to deal with. Did you know that there's a way to meet your financial goals and not have to deal with a bank? The next chapter is all about this important tip.

CHAPTER 11

BREAKING THE BANKS

The mansion was an amazing investment and my other properties proved to be fantastic as well. They were not always without their problems but, in the grand scheme of things, I was doing amazingly well and I was really getting ahead financially. Of course, I didn't see my journey ending with what I had. It wasn't long before I was combing the real estate listings webpage again, looking for more deals to add to my portfolio, and I was ready to do this by any means possible.

As will happen when you buy a larger, older home, you will have to spend a lot of money on maintenance, repairs, and projects. I spent some money as soon as I moved into the mansion, but that was more to make it income ready. Other expenses crept up. A large one was to replace the slate roof. Slate is often referred to as a lifetime roof, and this is true; however, what doesn't last a lifetime is the nails that hold the slate in place. The blacksmith nails (yes, they were that old—1873) were rusted through, and pieces of slate would go flying off the roof and land all over the yard. I was worried that these pieces of slate were like mini guillotines and might take out a neighbor, friend, tenant, family member, or Airbnb guest. The slate needed to be repaired.

I called around, but I couldn't find anyone who would work on slate. It was a dead art. I finally managed to get ahold of a company that would do the work, but what they told me was not something I wanted to hear. Just to repair the faulty sections of slate was going to cost six figures! That wasn't even to replace the entire roof. To fix the entire roof would have been triple the cost of repairing just the faulty sections.

My mind was made up. The slate had to go, and I was going to replace it with modern shingles. I ended up doing that and at a fraction of the cost to repair the slate. It still wasn't cheap, mind you, but it was a large roof with a lot of tall peaks. The repairs had to be done, so I went ahead with them. In the end, it looked fantastic and actually modernized the look of the home. The payback was not only increased equity from a new roof, but it also increased the equity by modernizing this wonderful Victorian gem.

The projects didn't stop with the roof. Parking was an issue. The driveway could accommodate up to four cars, but having multiple units posed a challenge. Often, the two-bedroom unit in the north wing had guests with more than one car. This was because two couples would sometimes book and arrive separately, or the booking was for corporate clients. Nearly 40 percent of our clientele was made up of out-of-town workers who needed places to stay. That meant parking was often in high demand.

For six months out of the year, parking wasn't a huge issue. We could park on the road to make room for our guests and tenants. The other six months, however, were an issue. The City had a no-parking bylaw in place from November to April so that the plows could come along to remove the snow.

To overcome this, I had to expand the driveway. I needed at least two more parking spaces. Our cobblestone driveway was gorgeous and really suited the house. I couldn't just pave a new section. Paving wouldn't match the feel of the home, it would look out of place and taint Airbnb guests' first impression when they arrived. I needed something different, but I didn't want to spend the time or money it would take to lay additional cobblestone. Realistically, even if I wanted to lay more cobblestone, it wouldn't have matched what was already there. It would look oddly different, but I wasn't about to invest in new cobblestone for the entire driveway just so it would match. I had just spent a ton of money fixing the roof earlier that year, so I needed a budget-friendly solution that would also be aesthetically pleasing.

Brigitte and I were mulling over what we should do, and she suggested using concrete. That was the perfect solution. It would look classy and distinguish the parking area so that we could direct guests to their assigned parking space. What a great idea! Now the problem was, where would we find a mason who could do the job? We needed someone reliable and not too costly to do the work. But where do you find someone like that?

In the age of the Internet, there has been a wonderful development in Facebook groups. We were members of the local neighbors' group and Brigitte made a post asking the other members who they recommended. One person's name came up a few times, so we called him to come provide an estimate.

When the mason arrived, I thought he was a pleasant enough guy. He was young and able, and had owned his masonry business for a couple of years already. I inquired as to where he learned the trade and he said he picked it up from his dad. That gave me the confidence that he knew what he was doing. We discussed the project and he showed me similar driveways that he'd done. The contractor recognized our need for a budget-friendly solution that would suit the grandeur of the home. He suggested stamped concrete. He showed me a few more pictures of driveways with stamped concrete and I was sold.

What a lifesaver this guy was! I couldn't wait to get this done. I let him know that it absolutely needed to be done before parking restrictions were in place. He told me he had a lot of clients but assured me that he could get the job done in time.

Weeks went by, and then a couple of months. I reached out to the contractor and asked him when he could squeeze us in. He was good about replying and came across as a pleasant guy. I am not one to get confrontational with contractors. I understood that he was busy, and I trusted that he would get the job done before November. I also like to keep good relations with contractors so that if I need them in the future, they are more than willing to work with me again.

After I sent a few more reminders to him, he came out the weekend that restrictions were to come into place. He showed up with a small crew and they got to work, stamped the concrete, covered it in raised plastic to keep it dry, and even put a heater under the plastic to encourage the concrete to dry properly. He pulled me aside and apologized for his delay and took full responsibility for the delay. He told me that he had called the City to inquire about purchasing an extended parking pass to allow us to park on the street for a few days. Unfortunately, the City didn't offer this sort of parking pass. Once the plows needed to run, cars weren't allowed to be parked on the streets overnight.

I was really impressed with the level of attention and care the contractor was putting into this. He not only called the City to find a solution, but he was going to pay for the extended parking permit out of his own pocket.

This was impressive. The fact I had to wait so long for him to do the job was also impressive. It meant that this guy was in high demand. This was someone I needed to hold on to as a good connection.

While dealing with the parking issue, I continued looking for ways to enhance my portfolio as an investor. I did find a cute little two-bedroom house with a great private yard. It had a sixties cottage type of feel. It was very cheap for a couple of reasons: It was small and a bit dated. It had only baseboard heating, as the old gas furnace no longer worked. The last issue was that it was right next to train tracks, which isn't ideal for most buyers. But I was not most buyers.

I saw that home and its potential. I saw the charm in the sixties cottage decor and immediately thought that I could turn this into another Airbnb listing. I really wanted this property, so I thought, how can I purchase this already-cheap listing for an even better price?

Then it came to me. I'd call the listing agent and arrange a viewing. She met me at the property and showed me around. She wasn't particularly good at her job, as she often stood back like I was wasting her time. I think she was expecting me to say after the showing that my agent would be in contact with her. Not only that, she really couldn't answer any of my questions. I thought, what a dud. They let far too many people become real estate agents without actually training them to be good ones.

Don't get me wrong, there are great real estate agents out there, but there are far more really crappy ones. She happened to be a crappy agent.

So, why did I bother continuing with this deal and talking with this agent? Strategy!

I said to the agent, "I like the home. It has potential, and I'm prepared to put an offer in." She was almost shocked. I continued, "I'm okay to have you represent both the seller and me. That way, you can double-end the commission." Her eyes lit up and I could see that this novice agent saw the color of money. She knew that, although this was the cheapest listing in our city, she stood to make quite a bit of commission by letting me structure the deal this way. Suddenly, she perked up and the glossy look in her eyes disappeared.

I told her my offer, which was well below the listing price. She said that her client wouldn't accept it, so I said, "Take it or leave it." She swallowed hard, but she was motivated to make my cheap offer work. She stood to gain huge by pushing my deal through.

She presented my offer with conditions of suitable finance and insurance to her client. Her client tried to counteroffer, but I refused it. I told the agent to tell her client that my offer was firm and final.

Another thing I had working in my favor was that the house had been sitting on the market for quite a while. The seller had listed it too high to begin with and it had already lost traction and interest from other buyers. More than ever, the crappy real estate agent was motivated to push my deal through. Her client didn't even want to respond to my offer, but the agent talked her into it. She convinced her that no other buyers were showing interest and that she had better take my offer, like it or not.

What a great strategy that turned out to be. I called my mortgage broker right away and said I needed to make this deal happen. I wanted to buy this property and turn it into an Airbnb. He did his thing and called around to the banks. He called me back and said he tried the big banks, but they didn't want to do the deal. I called the B lenders (credit unions and financial institutions that aren't banks) and they didn't want to do the deal either.

I was shocked. Why? I don't understand? This was literally the cheapest house in the city. After my down payment, I wouldn't even owe six figures. Why on earth would they not want to do the deal?

My broker said it was for a couple of reasons:

1. The property was right next to train tracks and lenders tend to shy away from that in the event of a derailment or some other issue caused by the trains.

2. They didn't like my debt-to-income ratio.

3. My income was insufficient.

4. Most banks and lenders don't finance under $100,000.

5. The banks and lenders would not finance an Airbnb.

What? Debt-to-income ratio? Okay, so I had used some line of credit to pay for some of the work that had just been done at the mansion, and I had some big-box store deferrals going on at the time. Those deferrals weren't coming due for over a year. And how could they say my income was insufficient? I was making so much money it wasn't funny. I had an amazing salary and I was making more than twice that as a landlord.

My broker said that they didn't see my debt as something I would pay off. They saw it as a total debt owed. And, as for my total income, they wouldn't count my Airbnb income and only 50 percent of the rental income.

I told him to have them look at my history of credit usage with my credit card as well as the deferrals from the big-box stores. I never paid interest. Not once. I paid my bills before they came due. And as for the income . . . that was ridiculous. If it was good enough for me to claim to Revenue Canada, it should be good enough for them to accept as income. I was certainly taxed enough on the income. They asked for my previous years' taxes. Why ask for that if they aren't going to factor it in?

My broker replied, "That may be true, but that isn't how the lenders see things. They see the line of credit with tens of thousands owing on it from the repairs."

I reminded him that my line of credit was a business expense. It wasn't like I went out and bought a luxury car or a boat with it. I couldn't let this deal go. It was too good of a deal. There had to be a way to make it happen. And as for not financing under $100,000, that was ridiculous. It seemed like they were trying to keep people in poverty.

My broker was sympathetic and said that, unfortunately, the banks can be a real pain to deal with. He didn't see an option with any of my traditional lenders.

I was dead silent on the phone for a minute. I had just structured and executed the perfect strategy to add to my portfolio and now the banks were about to pull the plug. This wasn't right and it wasn't fair. How could this possibly happen?

My broker then said, "I've looked at the numbers and you have a real solid purchase here. I don't see what the banks see; however, I have another option for you to consider, but it'll cost more than what the banks charge in interest."

I was excited and desperate to make this deal happen, so I was all ears.

He went on to say, "I deal with private lenders from time to time, and you're a perfect candidate to get a private mortgage. I've already presented your deal to one of them and they are prepared to finance it."

I replied, "Holy cow, that's amazing!"

I suddenly thought back to my landlord friend with the 200 units—the guy who reminded me of Tony

Soprano. He'd mentioned the same thing to me a while back and instilled the fear of losing my kneecaps.

I asked my broker, "Isn't that illegal? Aren't private loans mafia money?"

My broker laughed. "No, private lenders are regular people who like the security and return of mortgages. They look for deals like yours, which is why you're the perfect candidate. It will cost you though. Current private lending rates are 7.5 percent."

Wow! I couldn't believe it. My deal didn't have to die. Private lending was not some dirty back-alley thing that would result in "Vinny" and "Guido" paying me a visit in the middle of the night to pay up. A 7.5 percent interest rate wasn't bad . . . It was more than double what the banks charged, but I could still make a ton of money from this property at that rate.

So, being the brazen entrepreneurial Dutchman I was, I said, "Will you ask him if he will do 7 percent?" My broker said he would try.

He called me back and told me the deal would be financed at 7 percent, and the lender didn't care if I ran it as an Airbnb. How incredible! The banks said no, but I got to do the deal anyway.

You control your journey!

KEY READER TAKEAWAYS

Buying a property is not just an investment in the sales transaction. It requires ongoing investing. Often, as was the case with the mansion, you need to spend money to get a property income ready. In my case, I had to invest in creating and finishing the basement apartment, and that wasn't the only expense. I had to replace the roof, repair concrete around the in-ground pool, build an extension to the driveway, and hire an arborist to remove thirty-two unkept and overgrown trees, and move and repair a section of the wrought-iron fence to make room for the driveway extension.

All the maintenance, repairs, and renovations were necessary. There was no way of getting around them. They needed to be done and I had to have the capital available to do them. From an investment standpoint, everything I did had a great payback that increased the value of the property. You must budget for additional and ongoing expenses for your properties. Do not ignore or put off maintenance, repairs, or renovation needs, and find a reliable and trustworthy contractor to do the job. When you find great contractors, treat them right. Be patient and understanding and, above all, pay them right away. Yes, you can ride out the thirty-day requirement to pay a bill and even ask for extra time to pay the bill, but that's not how to maintain a good relationship.

When I get a bill from any contractor, I pay it immediately and so should you. Paying a bill as soon as you get it accomplishes several things:

1. It shows the contractor that you value their work and time.

2. It ensures that you don't forget to pay.

3. The contractor will be more than willing to work with you again.

4. The contractor may even shuffle clients in the future to work for you because they know you pay instantly.

5. It makes you more credible.

6. Contractors hang out with other contractors. Word will spread if you are a good or bad client. Be a good or even a great client.

7. You may also build a personal friendship. It is always good to have friends with skills.

Don't let the banks tell you no. I let them tell me no the first time I started seriously buying income properties. This stunted my growth for five years, and they tried to do it again when I wanted to move on the little property next to the train tracks. Their reasons were complete B.S.: Not funding under $100,000. Not factoring in certain income. Not liking my perceived debt to income ratio. Not liking the location. And not wanting to finance an Airbnb.

The banks will try to hold you back from achieving your financial goals and dreams. Private lending is a legitimate form of financing. It costs more but it's easier to get approved and saves the hassle. That alone is worth the extra expense. If your cash flow allows for it, do not negate this method of getting what you want.

Don't let the banks break you. You can break the banks!

CHAPTER 12
JOINT PAINS

There's a lot of talk about JV (joint ventures) in the world of real estate investing. You will hear the term in books, videos, podcasts, workshops, seminars, and conferences. They all paint a rosy picture and sell it as a fast-track way to success. I dipped a toe in the waters of JV and found it cold.

My relationship with the contractor continued, mainly because the mansion needed even more work. It was built in 1873 and still had the original lathe and plaster (nineteenth century drywall). It had gorgeous, artisan-sculpted crown molding all around, and beautiful artisan-sculpted medallions around each chandelier. It really looked like an antiquated fairytale home. We loved the look of these incredible handmade touches. Nothing was plain. Everything was ornate.

Our home inspired awe and wonder to all who walked through the doors. So much so, in fact, that our local arts council asked if we would consider showcasing our home as part of the Christmas Home Tour. Only six homes in our city were invited to participate, all grand mansions, and each home was paired with a designer and a florist to decorate it from floor to ceiling and room to room. We thought our home looked like something out of a fairy-tale before, but for the Christmas Home Tour, it became a whole other story.

We had so many people from the community walk through our home. They admired the decoration, the grandeur of the house, and all the artwork on the walls, which I happened to paint myself. Everyone loved seeing our home from the inside. The tour was a three-hour non-stop parade of people.

Leading up to this event, one thing caused us some concern. We'd noticed that part of the living room ceiling was drooping, so we both kept an eye on it. When we were getting our home ready for the tour, we got the ladder out to see the ceiling at eye level. There was no mistake about it. It had dropped over five inches. The sag began at the medallion of the chandelier and extended all the way to the handcrafted crown molding. This was about to become a drop ceiling and not the horrible designer kind you see in some homes or apartments. This baby was about to let loose.

What could we do? The Arts Council and the community were counting on our participation. The time that the designer and florist invested in bringing the space to life was a testament to their skill as well as a showpiece for them to gain more clientele. We couldn't pull out now.

While the Christmas Home Tour was under way, I kept nervously staring at the ceiling. I stood in the living room the entire time, greeting members of the community, and talking about our home and my art. People found it cool that I created all the artwork, so naturally, it was a great talking point. Let's face it, I've always enjoyed going to my own art exhibitions and meeting and talking with new people. This was my jam and I enjoyed every moment, but a little part of me was concerned that, with so many people walking through the home, the ceiling might give way. I stood in the living room as a host but also to ensure that I could clear it out quickly at the first sign of movement.

Thankfully, nothing happened during the Christmas Home Tour. The night was a success and the ceiling held fast.

I called my contractor buddy who did the driveway to find out if he knew anyone who could fix, repair, or replace the ceiling. He said that he did home renovations and was confident that he could take care of the ceiling. He came over, took a look, and couldn't believe the drop in the ceiling. He couldn't understand how the ceiling was still attached either.

He said it would be a big job, but he was confident that he could do it in about a week. Great! We hired him because we were impressed with his work on the driveway and he was a very likeable guy. We told him that the best time to do the ceiling would be while we went away for a week. We happened to be going on a trip to Cuba in two months' time. We asked him if he thought the ceiling would hold till then and if he could do the job while we were gone. He insisted that the ceiling would be okay for a couple of months and yes, he could do the job while we were away.

Cuba came and went. We had a great time and returned home to an unholy mess. There was dust throughout the entire house and the living room ceiling was gone. Lathe and plaster was everywhere. The ceiling ended up being a much larger problem than the contractor had originally thought. As it turned out, the only thing that was holding the ceiling up was the chandelier. Once he removed it, the entire ceiling collapsed. The floor wasn't damaged and, thankfully, we had moved out all the furniture.

When the ceiling gave way, it not only took the handcrafted medallion around the chandelier, but it also took the bulk of the crown molding surrounding the living room. The repair job ended up being a much bigger job than we first thought. But now what do we do? The other half of the living room still had its chandelier and sculpted medallion as well as the glorious, sculpted crown molding. There was no way this could be replaced and still look cohesive. The entire living room ceiling and crown molding needed to be replaced.

We decided to do something that suited the architectural style of the home and had the contractor make a custom coffered ceiling. This would look both modern and authentic. We may not have the sculpted medallions anymore, but we would still end up with a wow factor on our ceiling. We ended up getting modern chandeliers and wall sconces to flank the fireplace. The original sconces were damaged when the ceiling was removed. We modernized with a tip of the hat to the original design.

It took a few more weeks of construction, but in the end, the ceiling had that wow factor. Our home was gorgeous once again. The job wasn't perfect, as there were a few minor flaws but, overall, our contractor did a great job, especially for this being his first time doing a coffered ceiling in such a stately home.

I overlooked the minor flaws and enjoyed chatting with him throughout the process. He was young and determined. I really admired his work ethic and skill set, and we became friends.

A vacancy at my duplex came at the perfect time to convert the one side into two rental units. I asked my contractor if he thought I could separate and convert the front part of the unit into a one-bedroom apartment. He said it wouldn't be a problem. I hired him for yet another contract and he completed it very quickly and to great satisfaction. The place came out so nice that I would have lived there with Brigitte if we didn't have kids. It was a gorgeous apartment and I rented it to an elderly couple who were renovating their home. They were going to stay for at least six months.

I was so happy with my contractor's work that I brought up an idea with him. I suggested that we get into a flipping business together. He was intrigued. I said that I would buy the property and he could do the necessary renovations, and then we would split the profit on rent. He agreed, so we formed a corporation, signed the documents, and became 50/50 partners.

I found an amazing house. It was a large five-bedroom home with a two-car garage and a one- bedroom apartment on the second floor. We scoped this house and saw the potential. He looked at it through a contractor's lens and I looked at it through my creative, designer/artistic eyes. Together, we planned how to maximize this home's potential. I said I could get the funds for the down payment and secure the financing. He said he could finish all the work within two months. He was adamant that he would devote his evenings and weekends, or whatever it took to get the work done. What more could someone ask for in a JV?

The house was bank owned, and I employed the same strategy that had worked so well in my last real estate acquisition. I approached the listing agent and said they could represent both me and the seller to double up their commission. We went in with our offer and were so excited that it was accepted. We were on the tip of building something big.

I approached my bank about financing the property through the new corporation. They said they couldn't finance anything until we had two years of earnings under our belt in the corporation. I explained that, without financing, there wouldn't be any earnings. They said their hands were tied and their policy wouldn't allow them to loan anything to the corporation at this time.

So, I went back to my broker and asked if he would finance it. Once again, I was disillusioned with my bank. There I was making the most money I had ever made, and my net worth was ridiculously high, but the bank didn't want to finance. My broker shopped the deal out to all the A and B lenders, but they came back with the same issues. They were not willing to finance a new corporation. So, he did the next logical thing and found another private lender who would finance the deal. This time I would be paying 8 percent on the loan. I was okay with that, as my projections showed incredible cash flow. My partner trusted my judgment because I had done this successfully many times already. We took that deal and financed the home.

They say that the road to hell is paved with good intentions. This JV was a classic example of that proverb. Days turned into weeks, and weeks turned into months. The renovations weren't getting done. Every time I asked, there was always an excuse... his family, his kids, his wife, his contracts.

What happened to doing whatever it took? What happened to giving up every evening and weekend to complete the job inside two months? He installed a third bathroom right away, but after that, nothing else got done.

I was fed up. I had lived up to my end. I financed the down payment (with my line of credit, mind you). I told my partner that we needed to split the cost of the mortgage and he agreed, but he still wasn't out much money. Really, I was the only one who was hurting financially because of the delay. I couldn't recoup my initial investment to pay back my line of credit and had to make payments on it in addition to my portion of the mortgage.

Months went by and I kept asking when he would be able to work on our income property. He kept saying soon... this weekend... next week... in two weeks, I promise! None of that came to fruition. Desperate, I donned my work clothes and went over to do whatever I could. I decided to get the one-bedroom apartment finished so we could at least get the income going from that to cover costs.

I spent many hours working, tearing out carpet, removing carpet nails, refinishing floors, and painting. My partner was impressed with what I could do, but I was aggravated that I had to do it in the first place. That was not my role or responsibility. I had lived up to my end of the bargain while my 50/50 partner wasn't putting in his 50 percent of the work. We had a candid conversation and I expressed my dissatisfaction. He agreed that he'd let me and our partnership down and then insisted that he was going to prioritize the space.

To his word, he showed up to finish everything the one-bedroom apartment needed. I frequently went along to ensure that the work was getting done. I was this deep in already, I might as well continue to slug away at doing the necessary renos that were within my skill set. I was there more often than my partner and I was upset to see that my partner had sent his employees to work on the place.

This is not what we had agreed to. I was not financing that place and paying for work to get done on top of it. The deal was that he'd do all the work. My frustration continued, but I didn't say anything at this point because I just wanted the project done so we could make an income from it.

Brigitte was also frustrated because I was no longer at home and she felt like I was neglecting her and the kids. I explained that I needed to get this project done, even if I was doing the work I wasn't supposed to do. I was stressed, frustrated, and losing sleep, but it also wasn't fair that she had to deal with it. This compounded my stress and frustration.

Finally, we finished the apartment. I did about 70 percent of the work to complete the apartment. I also went out and bought all the furnishings for the place. I used my big-box store credit and got a fifteen-month deferral. The place looked so cute and it was Airbnb ready. The only problem was, who was going to do the cleaning and turnovers? Although this should have been my partner's responsibility, I couldn't count on him, and I knew that I would have no life if I had to do the turnovers.

I went back on the local listings website and found an ad posted by some out-of-town workers looking for a five-month lease on a furnished space. It was perfect! I called my partner and said he had the weekend to get the rest of the house ready, no ifs, ands, or buts! He agreed and finally put the effort in and, though the place wasn't fully renovated, it was good enough to rent.

I contacted the workers and offered to show them the place. Each room was incredibly large and each had a queen-sized bed. The living room had a lot of furniture and a flatscreen TV. Nice, welcoming art hung on all the walls, and the kitchen was fully stocked. There was plenty of parking for all of them, and the rent was way cheaper than the motel they'd been holed up in.

The boss and his wife took the upstairs apartment and his crew took the lower five-bedroom portion of the house.

We were finally making money. At least until the sewer backed up. I told my partner there was an emergency and he had to fix it. He said he didn't have time.

I was now losing my patience. "This is your job. Make the time." He got the message and rented equipment to repair it himself. It appeared to be a clogged sewer line, so he got a rotor and tried to clear it out. Things seemed to be fixed.

I got a call not even a week later. It happened again after a heavy rainfall. Clearly, it wasn't fixed. The workers were pissed and I didn't blame them.

This time my partner showed up with a plumber friend, so now the cost of a plumber needed to be paid. They worked on the line for quite some time before he told me what I owed his buddy. I lost it. I reminded him that I was financially responsible for the purchase of the house and that we were to share the profits, but it was his role to take care of any maintenance or repairs. Now, rather than living up to his responsibility, he hired someone at my expense. This was not how our arrangement was supposed to go.

Brigitte and I talked about how the project hadn't unfolded the way we had planned. In hindsight, I should have done the deal alone and hired him just to do the work. I would have been further ahead financially and the work would have been done right away. Brigitte suggested I buy him out, but I wasn't positioned to do that yet. I wanted to see if it would get better because I had so much hope that we could work the way we'd originally planned and eventually acquire more property.

It had been my goal to have at least three more properties under our JV partnership by now. We should have been able to renovate the current property, refinance it, get my capital back, and then use it to buy more real estate.

A couple of weeks later, the sewer backed up again. This time it cost us the workers who were renting the place. They said they couldn't put up with it and, frankly, I didn't blame them. They left and we were left with no income.

My partner said he didn't have time to fix the sewer, as he was in the middle of a big job. I was deflated. I decided to list the one-bedroom apartment as a full-time, fully furnished rental. I found a young paramedic who fell in love with the place and she agreed to rent it. It was her first place away from the home she grew up in.

At least we had regular income now. It wasn't as much as we received from the workers, but it covered costs. We weren't profiting, but we weren't losing either.

A little more time passed, and after more repeated requests, my partner finally showed up with large professional auger. He brought his plumber buddy along again, but I didn't say anything. I had already made my position clear on his role and responsibility. He chose to bring another contractor on board to do the work he was supposed to do.

After several hours, the plumber finally felt that he had discovered the issue. He said roots were likely growing in somewhere down the line beyond the reach of this largest piece of auger equipment. We would need to keep an eye on it. He gave me the invoice and I paid it . . . begrudgingly. I was pissed that I had to pay someone on top of cutting a 50/50 deal with my partner who was capable of doing this work. I was fed up, but I just wanted it done and over with so that I could recoup my investment.

This time we decided to list the five-bedroom unit on Airbnb. We got a booking right away from a guy who said he needed the space on weekends to spend time with his kids during his custody time. We thought it was a great deal—three people in a five-bedroom unit that would only be used on weekends.

Well, we were wrong. It turns out the guy lied. He booked it for a party. Neighbors called me, the tenant called me, and I called my partner. I told him to go over there for once and deal with things. He heard all the commotion and saw drugs out amongst a major mess. He told the guy that he was in violation of the house rules that we had posted on our Airbnb listing. The guy ignored him and closed the door.

All we could do was wait till the guy checked out the next day. When he finally left, we walked through all the mess and saw the damage. This was very disheartening. We finally had it income ready and it was a wreck again.

I was deflated and defeated. This whole venture had been a disaster from the get-go. I was in the losing position and my partner, with the minimal effort he'd put in, stood to gain. This was not how it was supposed to be, and it wasn't fair. I was not about to do another deal with him. I stopped looking at other opportunities to purchase, as this last straw was the one that broke the camel's back.

I turned to my partner and said, "Why don't you fix it up, we'll sell this property, and I will buy you out of the partnership." I played it like I was financially tapped. The truth was, I had it in me to keep going and buy more property, just not with him. I wanted out of the joint venture. He agreed.

No more JV for me!

There are many paths to success. Find the one that works best for you.

Key Reader Takeaways

I don't want you to think that joint ventures are not something to consider. There are many successful joint ventures out there and I haven't ruled out a joint venture in my future. I am not actively looking for a JV, but I would be open to the right opportunities.

It is extremely important to qualify what someone is bringing to the table in a JV. I thought I had found the perfect balance in the partner I picked. He was a lot younger than me, he was eager and hungry to get ahead, and he had an interest in real estate investing. My problem was taking him at his word about his performance.

Though I had seen how well he worked when he was contracted to do jobs for me, he didn't have the same attention and desire to focus on projects for our partnership. He chased his "paying" jobs and couldn't see that what we were doing was a paying job. If he had finished the work within two months, this investment would have earned him more than any contract he had going for him. Even at 50 percent, the potential rate of return would have been huge—both for this property and the future opportunities we'd have done together. We could very quickly have grown the business to a point where he may not have needed any other contracts, but it was not meant to be.

He lacked vision, insight, and commitment. That's what caused me to pull the plug on the partnership. If I did it again, I would build in performance incentives and requirements. His lack of commitment should have cost him, not me. I should have structured the JV so that he would lose shares if he didn't meet performance objectives. If he were to stretch a job out, he would no longer have been a 50/50 partner. I would have had the right to hire a crew to complete the work he was supposed to do, and those expenses would have been deducted from his share.

If you are going to consider JV, don't go in with blind faith. Speak with a lawyer. Get them to advise you on how to structure the partnership so that it is fair and equitable.

Build in performance clauses. That way things remain above board and are fair for both partners.

You will run into snags in your investment journey, but you need to find solutions to those challenges. Don't give up. You've got this!

CHAPTER 13

DOUBLE DOWN

No sooner had I spoken to my JV partner about selling the house and buying him out than I jumped on the realtor's website to find my next real estate opportunity.

I stumbled upon a great deal. I somehow always manage to find these diamonds in the rough at the end of the listings. This place was, once again, one of the cheapest properties in the city. It was a semi-detached house. Two separate tax rolls, which meant that they were more valuable.

One unit was quite run down. It had support issues on the main floor in the front part of the house. This wouldn't be a major repair, so no real cause for concern there. The other unit was more updated and had no support issues. I thought, Perfect! I will buy both. When it comes to semi-detached homes, I would rather own both sides than just one. You never can trust what another owner will do when your properties share a wall. For example, if their roof needed to be fixed and they neglected to do it, water would find the path of least resistance and wouldn't care about crossing a property line. My advice is to always buy both sides of a semi if you can.

I implored a tactic that had worked well before. I spoke to the listing agent and asked her to represent me as well as the seller. Then I could lowball both units and the agent would have incentive to push the seller to accept my offer.

I called the listing agent and offered just that and, to my surprise, she replied that they were an ethical real estate agency that was an arm of a law firm, and they did not represent both parties. This was the first time I met an agent who wouldn't represent both buyer and seller. I was shocked and impressed. She said she could show me the places, but that she wouldn't end up being my agent for the transaction. She offered to recommend an agent I could use. That was good enough for me.

I looked at both places. They were small, but very cute, and they were in one of the best up-and-coming areas near the waterfront. The agent told me that they had an accepted offer on the nicer unit, but the rougher unit was still available. I told her I wanted to buy both units or none at all. She said that the other offer wasn't great, and they only had until that night to release their conditions. This was my chance.

I still went in somewhat aggressive. My offer was less than what had already been accepted but I said I would pay the same for both sides. You may be wondering how I knew what the other offer was. It is true, real estate agents are not allowed to disclose the amounts of other offers. So, how did I come to find out? I happened to mention the property I was looking at to my business partner and he said, "Oh! My dad's offer was accepted on the one unit." He told me how much his dad's offer was and that he didn't think he would release his conditions in time.

How fortuitous! Armed with that knowledge, I went in $15,000 lower on my bid and stressed that if I could not buy both units, I was not interested at all. I got the call later that evening that my offer had been accepted. How awesome!

I was about to do it all over again. I contacted my broker and told him my plan was to turn it into two Airbnb units. He reminded me that the banks won't finance Airbnb. I already expected that, so I told him to find me private financing. I didn't care about paying double the interest rate on the places. It was an amazing deal that was going to create a massive cash flow.

Once again, I was getting ahead and my plan to expand my real estate portfolio was really coming together. I went home and told Brigitte that the offer was accepted and she was happy for me. She wanted to go see the places for herself. I called the listing agent again and asked her if she would mind arranging another walkthrough with Brigitte. The agent agreed and we toured both units a little while later.

The potential excited Brigitte. She knew it was going to be a moneymaker. I could see the wheels turning in her head, but she didn't say what she was thinking. We got home and she began talking about how cute and perfect those little semi-detached units were. Then she suddenly said to me, "I have an idea . . . Hear me out before you say no . . ." This sounded familiar, but the last time I heard those words, they were coming out of my mouth.

She went on to say, "What if . . . What if we moved out of the mansion, and into the one unit that needs work and then you can still earn the Airbnb profit on the other side?"

I was stunned. "Really?!? Are you serious? You want to leave this beautiful mansion to live in a tiny home?" The unit was just over 800 square feet.

Brigitte replied, "Yes, I'm tired of cleaning the mansion. It constantly needs work, and it makes you money on Airbnb anyway. Why not make it 100 percent Airbnb?"

She had a point. I really didn't care if we downsized. Quite frankly, I never thought she would want to leave the mansion. She was the one who said that we weren't allowed to move anywhere else.

It didn't take long for me to say yes. It was a great idea. The semi-detached was in a great area and had a huge lot. We decided that, since one unit was going to be on Airbnb, we would run a short wooden fence behind the back door of it to block out the backyard and that way we could take over both sides of the backyard. It would be great for the dogs, as well as the kids, and not to mention all the plants Brigitte loves to grow.

I told my business partner that I got an accepted offer on both sides of the semi-detached. He said that he didn't think his dad's deal would have gone through anyway and he was happy for me. I told him how impressed I was with the agent and that I thought we should use her to sell our joint venture house. He was shocked that she had the ethics to not represent both sides and agreed that we would use her and her law firm to close the deal.

I was second guessing holding onto the mansion as an Airbnb investment. It was fine to have the two smaller units running in the mansion (the coach house and the two-bedroom north wing). But the rest of the house was so immense that I worried about damage and parties, etc. I feared putting the five-bedroom portion of the main house on Airbnb because the custom finishes were so high end that I would never be able to find the craftspeople necessary to make repairs if guests got out of control. I decided to sell the mansion.

When the joint venture house was listed, I noticed some things about the realtor that gave me second thoughts. I wasn't very impressed with how she handled the listing or what she was willing to disclose to prospective buyers. I also wasn't happy about her lack of availability for showings. There were times when she asked me to open the place so she could show it. I thought that this was her job . . . why was I doing it? Isn't this why she gets commission? So, I decided not to give her the listing for the mansion.

I called a well-known agent who I'd been acquainted with in the past. He was more than happy to get the listing for the mansion. This was one if the nicest homes in the city and, when we listed it, it was the most expensive listing. It would be a special buyer who wanted it. Having such a large home isn't for everyone. Certainly, we had the track record to show how Airbnb could be used to pay for most of the costs.

I ended up closing on the semi-detached home in early March. We didn't move in right away, as we wanted to get some renos going first. I hired a contractor that I had used a few times before. He was great about doing all the required work before we moved in. It took a good six weeks from closing to complete the renovations.

The agent did a great job coordinating professional photos and videos of the mansion. That took about a week and then the listing went live. Instantly, we had requests for showings. We thought we would be able to sell quickly based on the immediate interest.

It was perfect because we didn't need to move any furniture from the mansion to the new place. We decided to buy all new furniture to suit that space. This way, the mansion would look lived in after we moved, and it would always be staged for showings. It also allowed us to move when we were ready.

Two weeks later, everything changed. The world changed. It was the year 2020. The COVID 19 pandemic was infecting people around the world at alarming rates and the government suddenly called for a lockdown. What the hell was going on? This wasn't part of the plan.

The lockdown put an instant halt in the market. There were no more showings. People were too scared. How would the rest of this play out? The lockdown continued beyond the two weeks it was supposed to. Now I had two properties that were just sitting. Thankfully, I was still able to host Airbnb guests who had booked prior to the lockdown. I hosted some long-term, out-of-town workers. Funds were still coming in to cover the costs, but the real estate market was dead.

Whatever interest there was in either property had completely dried up. We kept the listings active, but there was no real traction. Then restrictions started to ease. We were getting some interest on the joint-venture property, but only the odd inquiry about the mansion.

Eventually, the realtors realized that they would have to offer alternatives for people to view houses and started doing virtual walkthroughs. Interested parties would make an appointment and use their phones to FaceTime with the realtor as they walked through the space. Our joint-venture property realtor wasn't always available when clients needed her, so she asked me to shoot a video to use instead. I just wanted the house sold, so I complied, but how was this my job again?

Just when we were gaining momentum and receiving requests for property viewings after COVID-19 restrictions were lifted, the situation quickly reverted to a repetitive and frustrating cycle as if we were stuck in Groundhog Day. (For those who haven't seen the movie, it is about a cynical television weatherman who experiences the same day over and over again.) Once again, COVID 19 cases were on the rise. People were not abiding to lockdown orders and the disease kept spreading. This led to yet another lockdown, so naturally, the market came to a crashing halt. How in the hell were we ever going to sell these properties?

A few weeks later, the restrictions were lifted. Again. This time we had some good news. Some people who had looked at the joint-venture property just before the last lockdown were very interested. I told my partner that he needed to rush over there and fix up any little thing that needed fixing. Missing trim, paint, any open areas of walls, etc. He could have done that during the lockdowns, but he never put the time in to take care of those things. Again, no skin off his teeth.

Finally, we got a solid offer on the joint-venture property. We accepted it with the conditions of financing and inspection. No sweat. I told my partner again to rush over right away and take care of all the little things. He swore he would. Three days later, the inspector came and went, and the report came back. Vermiculite was visible in the open wall and the purchaser walked. Vermiculite is a form of insulation known to have asbestos in it.

I was livid. Had my partner listened to my repeated requests to go over and take care of little things like fixing the wall, this wouldn't have happened. He let me down once again. This time, it cost us the sale. I wasn't going to be able to recoup the investment. To make matters worse, he didn't seem all that put off by it. I would never enter into another joint venture without proper contractual obligations set. This could have been a major boost to my partner's life, but he didn't see it that way. I was glad to be buying him out of the corporation.

After the second lockdown, we got some traction on the mansion. One couple came through and it looked very promising. He was a new lawyer in town. They made their offer and we countered, and then they countered, and then we settled on a price. It wasn't quite what I wanted, but I was still more than doubling my money after only four years of ownership. Conditions included an inspection and financing. But hey, he was a lawyer . . . it should all be good, right?

As you can already tell, I had a lot going on in my life at this point and it was very stressful. After a couple of weeks of the joint-venture property sitting, we finally got another offer. It was a little higher than the offer that fell through. After all that hassle, it looked like it was finally going to sell. The inspection didn't come back with any issues. We disclosed that the last inspection found vermiculite, but we had closed the wall. The buyer's insurance said this was fine as long as it wasn't opened and disturbed. The buyer waived their conditions and we had a firm offer. Thank God!

After just over a year of owning the joint-venture property, the sale price was six figures higher than my purchase price. The property closed and the deal was done. I took the proceeds from the sale, paid myself back everything I'd put into the property, and with what was left, I had my accountant do a projected tax assessment of what the corporation would owe. Based on the accountant's calculations, about $30,000 was left over. I told my partner that his buyout would be $15,000 plus $1 for his share allocations. He accepted that. I cut him his check and was relieved to be done with the joint venture. No more of that for me!

Back to the mansion . . . I felt better knowing I had this money available in my corporation if I needed it. I also had solid bookings throughout the pandemic up until this point. Even when the government said that all short-term rentals were to cease operations, I had an exemption because I was housing workers. So, money kept rolling in.

I was feeling really good about the lawyer with an offer on the mansion. They had negotiated a good deal. We were throwing in a bunch of furniture. They did say that they were experiencing some delays due to the pandemic and asked for an extension to waive their conditions. I agreed. We wanted to work with them to keep the deal alive. We had no other offers or even interested parties. The pandemic had destroyed the housing market. Buyers retreated, so we wanted to work with the one we had.

After a couple of weeks of extensions, it came back that they were not able to get financing. I thought this was ridiculous. Why couldn't a lawyer get financing? For a couple of reasons: 1) As mentioned before, banks really do suck. Imagine giving a lawyer a hard time for a mortgage. 2) The lawyer was new to the practice. He had only graduated a year earlier. 3) He was deemed self-employed. This is what gets a lot of people. Good people are turned down by the banks all the time for these reasons.

My agent was desperate to keep the deal alive. He asked me to consider financing the lawyer with a vender take-back mortgage. This intrigued me. Hmmmm. I could sell the mansion and finance it back to the lawyer and still make money from it after the sale. This seemed quite interesting. Only two years earlier, I was borrowing private money to buy a home and had used private funds for three more properties since. Now I was about to become a private lender. How cool was that?

I thought long and hard about it and, ultimately, decided that I did not want my first exploration into the world of becoming a private lender to be on the mansion. That would have been a large amount of money tied up in one deal. I also had plans for my other properties that I needed the funds for. I called my agent and told him the deal was dead.

Lockdown number three came. After about six more months of the mansion just sitting on the market, I really began to worry. I was losing sleep once again. Brigitte could tell I was not happy. I loved the plan we had for the semi-detached home we were living in, but I was really stressed about the mansion. The market was starting to pick up and we noticed properties were selling for much more than what we thought they were worth. I finally said to Brigitte, I think the mansion is too expensive of a house to sell right now. People aren't comfortable spending that kind of money during these uncertain times. Cheaper homes are the ones selling like hot cakes. Maybe we should consider moving back into the mansion and selling the semi-detached home.

Brigitte wasn't happy, but she knew the stress I was under. So, she decided to ask the kids. They were the ones who were going to be uprooted once again. They loved their bedrooms in the semi-detached. They each had two levels in their rooms. A lower level, and then attic stairs that led to a loft where they slept. Their rooms were bedrooms and living rooms all in one. Brigitte was sure they would not want to leave the semi-detached.

We called the kids over and Brigitte began to speak. "Hey guys . . . what would you say if . . ."

Then our daughter interrupted and blurted out, ". . . We moved back to the mansion?" What a smart kid. How did she know? Brigitte conceded that we were moving back. The kids were super excited. We told them we would only move back if we could sell the semi-detached house. They understood.

We called an agent and asked her to list the semi. It was up for just one week and we accepted two offers. These offers were double what I had paid for them less than a year earlier. The closing date was set for the one side. It was exactly one year to the day that I had purchased it. How incredible. One year and I was more than doubling my money. The stock market would never have done this for me. I was ecstatic!

This was an insane time in my life. So much was going on. So much stress. And yet, so much peace and comfort knowing that we were doing amazingly well financially. I was in a good position before, but after that I was in a whole new category of financial freedom.

You need to be both patient and resilient. Your goals are within sight!

KEY READER TAKEAWAYS

There are a few lessons to be learned here. The big one is that you can never plan for the unexpected. The unexpected will arise in so many ways. It could be an issue with a unit you own. Perhaps a new roof or major plumbing issue. Those issues can arise out of nowhere, but you can sort of plan and prepare for such events. Who would have ever guessed that a pandemic would shut the planet down? It seemed as though our society should have been way too technologically advanced to be taken down by a microscopic organism. I certainly never thought it was possible.

The pandemic shook a lot up. At first, it killed the market entirely. Then the market bounced back with a vengeance. Properties skyrocketed. This lesson taught me to be adaptable. I had to adapt and make the decision to move from the mansion to a small semi-detached unit and then, as the pandemic went on, adapt to moving back into the mansion to sell the semi-detached.

This was a lot in a short amount of time, but the fact that I more than doubled my money in exactly a year led me to make a drastic shift in my real estate investment career. I pivoted from wanting to accumulate more properties to wanting to capitalize on the insane market and sell virtually all my property. Again, I credit my amazing partner and her openness to consider what was best in the big picture. She had blind faith in my decisions and financial moves and was willing to follow my lead.

Be cautious when heading into a joint venture, as JVs can end in disaster if all aspects aren't accounted for. I will never enter into a JV again unless there are contractual stipulations about performance and expectation. If my partner stood to lose shares for his lack of action, he would have been motivated to see the project through. Make a solid contract before entering a JV. Think twice before considering a JV.

There's a lot of knowing when to hold 'em and when to fold 'em. The unexpected can be a great time to pivot your direction. Be open to opportunity!

CHAPTER 14

LENDER BENDER

What an absolutely crazy time in life. Not only was the world in upheaval from the pandemic, but suddenly, everything was increasing in value and demand. Especially in the world of real estate. Nobody would have predicted the complete and sudden halt in the real estate market. Then, soon after, nobody could have predicted the insane increase in demand for real estate.

Everything in the market began igniting and exploding. Valuations were going through the roof. Just when we thought the market had peaked, it went higher and higher.

This turned into new opportunities. My focus on accumulating real estate had now shifted. I had a lot of money in the bank from the sale of several properties. I decided it was time to segue in to becoming a private mortgage lender. I knew the drill. I had borrowed privately for a few of my properties in the last three years. I knew what kind of interest I was paying. I was making someone else rich and they had no obligations whatsoever. It was my time to capitalize and become a private lender.

I started off easy. I approached one of my tenants who had expressed an interest in buying the house if I ever chose to sell. He was not in a position to get conventional financing. His credit wasn't the best and he'd been a lifelong renter. He did come into some money after his mother passed away, so I knew he had a down payment.

I approached him and asked if he was interested in doing a private deal. I explained that the interest rates were much higher, but it would get him in the market and he wouldn't have to deal with banks. He was all over the deal. I felt I had nothing to lose. I owed less than $100,000 on that house and could sell it to him for nearly triple what I had owning.

I made an appointment with my broker and told him my plan. He thought it was great. I also don't think he ever thought I would move so quickly from private borrower to lender. Even I didn't expect events to turn so quickly.

My broker set up the deal. I wanted to capitalize on a good, strong down payment, so I helped my tenant get information on government grants for first-time home buyers. With the help of my broker, we talked to that arm of the government and got my tenant approved for the grant that amounted to 5 percent of the purchase price. My tenant was ecstatic that I had helped him get access to free money. It was great to be able to help him out, but helping him out also helped me out. It put a larger down payment in my pocket and assured me that my tenant wouldn't walk away from the deal so easily. I didn't want to have to seize the property back if he wasn't able to make the payments. So, this gave a greater sense of security.

There's something you need to understand about how private lending works, especially when it comes to selling and financing a property you already own. What made this the perfect deal for getting my feet wet was that there was very little money left owing on the property. In order to legally finance a private mortgage on a property you already own, you must own it outright. A mortgage can't be tied to the property.

Knowing this, I took some of my newfound wealth and completely paid off my mortgage. This was the first time I could claim to be mortgage free on any property. What an accomplishment! If the deal fell through, I was content to refinance the property at conventional rates and use the excess funds to help pay off other properties. I had a Plan B. Thankfully, I didn't need it.

I created an agreement of purchase and sale (APS) and presented it to my tenant with all the terms and conditions. He accepted them and signed the APS. It was now firm. I hooked my tenant up with a lawyer I had used in the past. He also appreciated that. I was really helping him navigate everything that was necessary for him to take ownership of the home.

What was cool about this deal was that, once I paid off the $83,000 that was still owing on the mortgage, I could act as private lender. I sold the property for nearly quadruple the amount. Plus all the years that I made income off of it on both Airbnb, student rentals and now as full-time rental to my tenant who was about to become a homeowner.

The date of the closing came and, with a stroke of a pen and a $75,000 down payment, I became a private lender. My former tenant was happy. Although, he was paying more each month than when he was renting from me, he was pleased as punch because he was now a homeowner.

So, I increased my cash flow, increased my assets (loans are considered assets) and launched myself ahead in the world of private lending. This was a good, cheap property to test this out on and everything was fantastic.

Now I wanted to do it again. I loved how I had manufactured money and wealth out of thin air. Paying off a property that had significant equity built into it was an amazing way to begin this new focus on real estate investing.

I approached another tenant in a different house. This house was significantly more expensive and would take a lot more to pay off. I didn't have enough cash to do it, so I needed to get creative.

I went back to my broker and told him my new plan. In order for this plan to work, I had to refinance my large semi-detached duplex I bought ten years prior. He called up an appraiser and the appraiser came to do his thing. At the end of it, I was not happy with the numbers. I said the appraiser was completely out to lunch, but didn't delay, as I was focused on closing another sale that I would privately finance.

I accepted the low appraisal and used those funds, plus what I had leftover in my bank to pay off my other property. I approached that tenant and she said she was very interested in doing the private deal.

We agreed on a price. I sold it to her for the most she could afford. I could have sold it much higher to another buyer but, in the end, I stood to make a lot of money off the property just by virtue of being the private lender. The other reason I chose to sell it to my tenant cheaper than market value was because she had modified a lot of things in the home, without permission. She had foster kids and needed extra bedrooms. She chopped up the basement of that five-bedroom home and added four more bedrooms. This boosted her foster-care income, but it definitely lowered the property value. I wanted to make sure the deal would work with her because I didn't want to have to try to fight a legal battle to have her restore the house to its original condition. Who knows how that would have ended up. It could have gotten really messy.

I paid off the mortgage on that home and was happy to be mortgage free on another home. Again, this was quite an accomplishment. Not that long ago, I was in debt seven figures, but now I was in a position to pay off some of my real estate. It felt good. Amazing, actually, because I could still hear all the naysayers who thought I was insane for getting into real estate as an investment. I had proven them all wrong, and the timeframe between being deep in debt to having mountains of cash was not that long.

There was a point during refinancing and paying off the mortgage that I thought my tenant was going to pull a fast one. She was having issues coming up with the down payment. She asked to prolong the closing date. I thought she was trying to back out of a firm deal and had no interest in letting her do so. I asked her how much she was short and she stated that it was a lot. I lowered the down payment to just 3 percent of the purchase price. I wasn't about to let her come into the deal without any skin in the game, especially since I suspected she might back out.

What my tenant didn't realize was that, as an owner, she didn't have as many rights as when she was a tenant. She still thought like a tenant, but I treated her like an owner. We had a legally signed deal that she could not back out of. Even though I was getting less money upfront, I would more than make up for the decreased down payment with the increased monthly payment I would be getting from her. Besides, if she were to default on the mortgage, I could have the property seized and back in my possession a lot sooner than if I had to deal with her as a tenant in the landlord and tenant tribunal.

When all was said and done, I had quadrupled my money on that property, too. I went back to my broker and told him that I wanted the semi-detached appraised again and that I was willing to move lenders. It had been about three months since the last appraisal and refinance.

The new appraisal was ordered and it was nearly $200,000 higher than the previous valuation. I knew that appraiser had been out to lunch. I was vindicated! I took that appraisal and refinanced the duplex again. I wanted to use those funds to renovate the duplex, plus I was going to have a ridiculous capital-gains tax hit from selling off all my property. More on this later.

The deal finally closed on the other privately financed home and, once again, my tenants couldn't have been happier, even though they were now paying an extra $1,300 a month in mortgage payments than rent (because of the private-lender interest rate). They were homeowners and they were happy. I helped them when a bank wouldn't.

The deal wasn't a perfectly smooth one. They did try to act like tenants several months into their ownership. The mortgage payments were late. I immediately sent them a letter stating that penalties and interest charges needed to be paid. They were still used to being tenants. Tenants can be late with the rent and no interest or penalty charges apply. Now, they had to pay hundreds of dollars on top of the monthly payment. They were quick to make arrangements and got the loan back in good standing. This was an expensive lesson for them. This also made them want to get out of the private loan as soon as possible. Which was fine with me.

Several months later, I got a call from my broker. The borrowers had the house appraised and it was valued much higher than what I had sold it to them for. No surprise there. So, they found a conventional lender who was willing to finance them. No problem! For them to get out of the private mortgage, they were going to have to pay me three months' interest as a penalty.

When that deal closed, I was shocked to realize that, after paying me mortgage payments for only eight months, three months' interest amounted to more than the original loan amount! That's right! I made more money from them in that time. This was a major perk to being a private lender.

Once again, I had mountains of cash in the bank. I liked it and I didn't like it. It was a nice change after seeing a seven-figure debt. I literally could go out and buy properties with cash if I wanted to. But that wasn't what I wanted.

After talking it over with Brigitte, we realized that the out-of-control market had once again made properties like our mansion a suitable candidate to sell. Not only had valuations increased exponentially, but the expensive houses were now selling for cash offers, no conditions, and quite often, for more than the asking price.

I turned to Brigitte and said that this may be the perfect time to sell the mansion. I really felt that if we didn't try to sell it now, we may regret it down the road. This progression of an out-of-control real estate market wouldn't continue forever.

We listed it again. This time for hundreds of thousands more than we had listed it just one year prior. The activity was instant and there was a lot of interest. Within one week, we had an all-cash offer on the table. Seven figures! The only condition was an inspection. We likely could have held out and possibly gotten a couple hundred thousand more, but this was a good offer as it was. We made five times the money we paid only five years earlier.

We accepted the offer without having a place to move into. It was ironic. I was a real estate investor, a private mortgage lender, and yet I was homeless. We gave notice to the tenants on one side of the duplex so we could go owner occupied.

I created an elaborate financial incentive for that tenant to vacate ASAP. For each month he could leave earlier than the date we needed the unit, I was willing to pay him thousands of dollars.

We ended up in an Airbnb after the sale of the mansion. When the tenant finally left and we saw the state of the unit, we knew we wouldn't be moving in anytime soon. We needed to do a full gut and reno.

Things rarely go according to plan. Do your best and then learn to roll with the punches!

KEY READER TAKEAWAYS

Have a plan, but be open to modifying it. It is good to have a vision, goals, and a roadmap to where you are going. Sometimes, the best results come after deviating from your roadmap. I always like to think of the poem "The Road Not Taken" by Robert Frost.

> *Two roads diverged into a wood and I —*
> *I took the one less travelled by,*
> *and that has made all the difference.*

There is such wisdom in those words. One road was not better than the other. The two roads presented a choice and, for Robert Frost, making his choice made all the difference. Be open to taking the road less travelled.

A theme that keeps surfacing is to be creative. Time and time again, I come back to the fact that you need to think outside of the box and find solutions to challenges. I don't like to think of the situations I come against as problems. A problem isn't so easily fixed. A challenge, however, is just begging for a solution.

When my tenant was ready to purchase my home, I did whatever I could to help him out. I worked within his budget. I hooked him up with government incentives. This benefited us both. It helped him achieve the dream of homeownership and gave me greater security with respect to how much money he was able to use for a down payment.

The down payment was necessary to ensure that my tenant had skin in the game as well as for the practical aspect of giving me the funds necessary to deal with the inevitable—taxes! There seem to be more benefits to how capital-gains taxes are treated in the USA. In Canada, the government wants its piece of the pie and it wants it up front. In the USA, my deal would have deferred the capital gains over the life of the loan. Wherever you live, get to know the laws and rules. If you don't know where to start, speak with a qualified chartered accountant. Do not seek advice from family or friends. Go to the experts!

Creative solutions to challenges sometimes require you to think ahead and strategize based on what could happen in order to prevent the collapse of a well-structured deal. I knew it would be more challenging to pull the private mortgage lending off with my tenant with the foster-care business. Once she agreed and signed the APS, I wanted to keep that deal alive and see it through.

I did whatever I could. I re-mortgaged a property that I'd only financed three months earlier. I took a gamble on the fact that the new appraisal would come out much higher, because I knew the market. I knew the trends and where they were headed. I made sure that deal went through. I took a lower down payment in order for the ownership to change hands and so I could continue profiting off that property as the private lender.

I often spend my free time on the real estate website to keep on top of what is happening in my city. At any given moment, there's a good chance I could tell you how much any house is listed for, what agent has the listing, and whether the house had dropped or increased in price. I may even be able to tell you the last time that house sold. Know your industry! Research!

When you pivot and enter the world of private lending, you really do feel like a bank. In fact, the term for private lenders is called *shadow banks*. It sounds so shady and clandestine. Truthfully, the only shady and clandestine part about it is that you realize how surreal the world of money is. Money comes into existence through the creation of debt.

By taking assets I already owned and using them as a vender take-back mortgage, I created money and value out of nowhere. Beyond the valuation for the sale, the money kept being generated monthly as a result of the ongoing debt that required servicing. The monthly mortgage payments became the best cash-flowing investment. I made more money each month holding the loans than I did as a landlord. I also had zero responsibility to the properties. There was no worry of a roof that needed fixing, a tenant who was late on rent, a sewer backing up, or any other problem that can arise with owning a rental property. It is worry-free investing. Now I know why banks love mortgages so much.

Being a private mortgage lender may not be something you are planning as part of your investment journey, but be open to the possibility. I encourage everyone to consider this as an investment strategy when the time is right.

Another theme in this book has been adapting to changes in my own personal living situation. Be willing to shift and move between properties in order to maximize returns. I lived in several of my properties on several occasions. You don't need to feel stuck in your own home. Just because it's your primary residence doesn't mean you shouldn't consider moving into one of your other investment properties. Your home can easily become another investment property, or you could sell it and use the proceeds to further your goals. Don't get stuck in your home the way people get stuck dealing with the same bank or insurance company. Switching things up can save and make you much more money.

Have your plan, begin your investment journey, but be open to change. Your financial future is within your grasp. Make the move!

CHAPTER 15
DOWNSIZING AND SEVERING

A lot happened in a short amount of time. The world shut down, opened up, shut down, opened up, shut down, and opened up again. The resulting tidal waves created a lot of upheaval in the real estate market. The chance to pivot and cash out had never been stronger.

After selling the mansion, we wanted to downsize in a major way. We needed a new home within walking distance of the kids' school, and we wanted to learn to live with less.

We sold our mansion at the peak of the market. We almost couldn't have timed it better. The market peaked three months after we sold, and then it dropped. House prices declined as much as 20 percent after the Bank of Canada decided to drastically raise interest rates. We felt so at peace with our decision to sell.

We had cash in hand and were ready to make our next purchase. The problem was, once we began looking for a house, we were still within that three-month range of where the market was still going crazy.

I had never had so much money in my life and yet I felt defeated when it came to trying to buy a home. I was that guy going into houses and offering all cash, $100,000 over the asking price with flexible closing. What more could a seller ask for, right? Wrong!

My overly generous offer was not working in this crazy market. I had bid on at least half a dozen homes and not one offer was accepted. Who were these insane people bidding against me and where had they come from?

The pandemic created a mass metropolis exodus. People realized the pros of living in smaller communities. Their buying power was huge and, thanks to the demands of remote working, the requirement to be in a city for work no longer existed. Technology had changed the world. If the pandemic had happened even five years earlier, it would have been much more devastating for the economy.

People could do their jobs from anywhere. They also realized that their house values were insane in big city centers. They were insane everywhere, but the prices in smaller communities were extra insane because big-city people were cashing out in favor of living in a small community. This created the largest influx of cash buyers the world of real estate had ever seen. Lucky me . . . I got to compete with them to purchase a home.

We were getting desperate. None of my offers were accepted and I couldn't stomach offering so much more to buy a house to beat out the big-city buyers. We were very rich and very homeless. What a juxtaposition! We were not on the street, but we were living in an Airbnb. We lived there for five months before we finally bought a home.

We ended up finding an off-market deal. It was a newly renovated bungalow. The seller hadn't even finished renovating the house. The basement was completely unfinished, but the current owner had plans to build a one-bedroom apartment in it. We saw the value of this and said that we would buy the house for the asking price. We told the owner to continue with soundproofing the basement ceiling and roughing in the plumbing for the kitchen, but to not install it.

The basement would end up being a perfect place for our kids to hang out and have their own bedrooms and space. As teenagers, they were in love with this idea.

The house was quite a drastic change. The mansion was over 6,700 square feet, and each floor of the new house was only 888 square feet.

We definitely loved the decluttering aspect of our life. We downsized in a major way and instantly learned to live with less. Managing a smaller home was so much easier than the mansion.

We had goals and dreams of living on a yacht in the Caribbean after the kids finished high school and moved out. Downsizing was in preparation for what we hoped our future had in store for us.

In the meantime, work was underway to completely gut and renovate the one side of my semi-detached duplex. Everything was stripped back to bare brick and built new. The process came with some hiccups. Good help can be really hard to find. We ended up with contractors who were trying to take advantage of us. It wasn't that they weren't hard or fast workers, but their quotes were so outrageous that we called them on it.

They didn't like that we were questioning the quotes and invoices. They also didn't like that we were questioning the legalities of how they were double-charging taxes on subcontracted work. It didn't take long for that relationship to be severed. We felt good that we were not going to be taken advantage of anymore, but now there was the challenge of trying to find new contractors during a pandemic fraught with supply-chain issues and a runaway increase in building costs.

I may have had more money than ever but, holy cow, were things getting ridiculous in cost and quality! Supply-chain issues and access to skilled labor grew exponentially. Inflation was out of control, but the show had to go on. I needed to get this reno completed.

After a few weeks of nothing getting done, I found some guys who would do the work. They were trained as builders in the military and knew their stuff. They were full-time military laborers and would do my work on evenings and weekends. This moonlighting relationship worked out well. Their rates were reasonable, the work was good quality, and there seemed to be few issues.

A few months later, both laborers left the military to start their own renovation business full time. Once they no longer had steady paychecks, I noticed that their rates increased. I understood the need to make a living, but increasing rates just because they quit their jobs wasn't sitting well with me. I went with it because alternatives were lacking, and I had a desire to just get the renovation done.

Their rates weren't all that became an issue. They were now taking on all kinds of work and spent less and less time on my job. In fact, as the weather improved and got warmer, they completely abandoned my job in favor of doing outdoor work.

The show must go on. I continued with my other plan for that property. The fact that it was a semi-detached home under one title bothered me. I always had the intention of severing it into two separate properties. It was built as two residences but had clearly merged into one title at some point over the last 150 years since it had been built.

The reason I hadn't severed it earlier was because I'd be required to run a new water and sewer line. That was an expense I'd set aside for the future. Since I now had the money, I felt the time was right.

Severing is the legal process to have a property like the semi-detached recognized as two individual properties. This allows one to be sold while the other is retained.

Severing the semi-detached would instantly add a couple of hundred thousand dollars in value to the property.

My severance was granted with the conditions that I get the separate sewer and waterline installed and acquire an updated survey of the property. I got on both right away. I contracted an excavation company that did that type of work and could do it within a month. I ended up waiting a few more months for the surveyor. Everything related to real estate was backlogged.

My contractors, who had abandoned the job for three months, called me out of the blue. They were ready to continue. I was now livid. I had already overpaid them for the work they did. I was the first big contract to hire them while they were still in the military. I dealt with the fact that they refused to provide invoices and would accept cash only. I turned a blind eye to all of that because I just wanted to get it done. I reached out a few times and there was always the promise that would start next week. Next week never seemed to come. My property sat for three months until they were finally able to start working.

I'd had enough! I told them not to bother coming. I no longer cared about getting the renos done, as it had dragged on for over nine months, three of which they made no progress whatsoever. I needed the renos to get done, but these guys weren't getting another dime from me.

Their final bill was a total slap in the face. They quadrupled their rate as a big F.U. Fine. I normally pay invoices the day I get them because I value the workers I hire. This time, they were desperate for cash, as they had no other alternative for employment. I sat on their invoice for exactly thirty days, as is allowed by law. F.U. right back. Another F.U. that I had in my back pocket was that I kept detailed records and texts about the job. I had every intention of claiming all the cash jobs that they forced me into and fully report their tax evasion to Revenue Canada. F.U. again guys!

I made friends with a couple of guys who did renovations over the summer. When I fired my contractors, I immediately let my friends know that the job was theirs if they wanted it. They thanked me and were very eager to take on such a big renovation. They agreed to do the work for less than half the cost of the crew I had just let go.

Finally, that project was coming together. My severance was approved. I met the conditions that were required for the approval. The last step was the land survey.

That finally got completed and filed five months later. It was now January 2023. When I'd made my application to the City for severance and a minor variance, I had used a survey that was on file from the 1970s. It turned out that there was a discrepancy between the approved measurements compared to the measurements indicated on the new survey.

The discrepancy was off by 0.3 meters. This was a big enough difference that it forced me to apply to the City again to get the new measurements recognized as part of the approval for the severance. Of course, I had to pay the filing fee again and, of course, because it was a new year, the filing fee went up from $750 to $1,150. That was a big jump, but I had come too far now to let such a little thing hold me back. I paid the $1,150, got my case date, made my presentation, and in less than two minutes, it was all approved again.

My rush to get the severance done didn't work out as planned. Rushing and using an old survey cost me more time and money. Hopefully, you can learn from my mistake.

When you look at it though, I had now created a new house where one hadn't existed before (on paper). It cost me less than $30,000 to complete the requirements to make this an income property. That is a pretty good rate of return, I would say. If you get a chance to buy a semi-detached property under one title, do it and sever it. It is so worth it!

When you are dedicated and persistent, you will see the payoff!

KEY READER TAKEAWAYS

Read the market and make determinations quickly as to what the right course of action is for your real estate investment journey. In my case, cashing out and selling most of my property made sense. For you, it might make better sense to accumulate more property, or to hold on to what you have, or to reinvest in what you already own.

Perhaps look into adding more units where permitted. Lock in your interest rate(s) when you see them on the rise. The exponential hike in interest rates caught many investors off guard and left them with properties that weren't generating income. Having said that, those investors had their heads buried in the sand. The spike in interest rates came as no surprise. Economists were preaching that the low-interest rate era wouldn't last. They talked about rising interest rates for years.

Use a clear head when planning your journey and look at all sources of information. Take a balanced approach to investing.

Learn to live with less. We felt great when we downsized from our mansion to our tiny home. This also extends to your lifestyle. While you are growing your portfolio, resist the temptation to get that fancy new car. Learn to be content. Let your investments grow and reinvest your profits back into your business. If your goal is to retire early, don't prolong it by spending money. Make your money work for you, don't work for your money!

Don't be afraid to make decisions that may seem to be counter intuitive. During my reno of my semi-detached duplex, I had to fire two different crews. I should have been quicker to fire the second group of contractors.

Instead, I waited three months while nothing was getting done before pulling the plug.

Relationships with contractors should be built over time. It takes all parties involved to foster and grow a relationship. If your contractors aren't going to respect you or the work you bring them, if they slack off and take on other jobs when they should be committed to your project, then cut ties right away and move on.

I am more than fair with my contractors. I treat them well and have complete respect for them. I pay them the day I get an invoice. I want my contractors to feel valued and appreciated, but I expect the same in return.

Don't cut corners when it comes to renovations or legal processes. The mistake that cost me time and money was rushing my application for the severance and minor variance. I used an old survey on file and that cost me. Had I waited until I had the new survey, I would have saved time and money. In the grand scheme of things, it wasn't a huge amount of time or money, but money is money and time is money. I lost both in this process.

When assessing the potential of investment properties, look for elements such as: semi-detached, extra land size, potential to add more units, separate entries, and parking. These are all items that you can easily get by applying to the municipality and making your case. They are incentivized to work with you. It looks good when a municipality can claim to have added greater housing density, especially in a housing shortage.

Though I began my investment journey more than thirty years ago, the real intense focus happened in the last thirteen years. That is a really short time to have amassed millions of dollars, and I did it all with twelve units, which isn't a huge amount in the grand scheme of things, but it was enough to provide me with financial freedom and security. I can say, without a doubt, that I would not have been able to do what I did on the stock market. What I did was pretty incredible. I leveraged debt and used it wisely. There are plenty of stupid ways to use debt, don't fall into that trap.

Debt creates money. I created money and wealth by understanding debt and using it as a tool to get ahead. If your journey is just about to begin, or has only just begun, I want my story to encourage you. My financial path worked well for me, and it is my hope that has inspired you to remain focused and invest in yourself and your future. Begin your journey today!

CHAPTER 16
FATHERLY ADVICE

This book was written to be an inspiration and encouragement for newbie and wannabe investors. I have chronicled my financial journey in hopes that it has provided a glimpse into how you can be successful with real estate investing. My journey isn't complete, but I have accomplished a lot so far. It is worth sharing now.

I can't tell you how many times I've had friends, family, and colleagues stop and ask me how I did it. They say I make it look so easy. The reality is that it is simultaneously easy and not easy. It is my hope that you learn from my mistakes, hesitations, and perhaps even through some missed opportunities.

My journey has been very successful. People constantly comment that I have a horseshoe up my ass. Perhaps luck had a little bit to do with it, but the reality is that I built everything I have from the ground up. I did so by surrounding myself with others who were successful at it. I was a sponge. I learned by asking questions, and through observation and research. I calculated risks and those risks paid off.

Begin your journey right away. I had my wandering years when I did not pursue real estate investing. If I truly began my journey at age twenty-one, I would have made millions more and much sooner. Along with that, don't accept no from anyone, especially the banks. When the banks told me to stop, I listened. I didn't know about private financing. Had I been open to that opportunity sooner, I would have accelerated my success.

Find the right relationship partner. Someone who will share your goals, vision, and passion, and encourage you in your journey. Brigitte has been a tremendous source of encouragement. She shares the vision and now makes the suggestions that may have already been brewing in the back of my mind. We complement each other well on all levels! I was in a relationship that was not so supportive and that really did hold me back. Share your journey with the right person.

When you achieve success, give back! Be open to encouraging other investors. Volunteer in your community. Donate to worthy causes. Be philanthropic. Coach little league. Serve on boards and committees. Make your community a better place.

So how do I encourage my kids? First, I recognize their strengths and abilities. What works for my son doesn't work for my daughter, but the truths we teach them are equally apportioned. We speak openly about finances, successes, struggles, and failures. Too many people avoid discussing finances. They treat it like it is something dirty that should be discussed only behind closed doors.

We want our kids to be financially literate and have worked hard to impart these lessons beginning at a young age. We taught them about different types of bank accounts and the importance of saving instead of spending all their money. We encourage them to earn money and reward themselves in carefully thought-out ways.

You don't want to feel like you are a slave to money. If you don't reward yourself, you will feel like you are doing it all for nothing. True, the ultimate reward is to be financially independent and to take an early retirement, but if that goal feels too far in the future and is intangible, you may lose sight and feel like it isn't paying off.

My fourteen-year-old daughter doesn't have a desire to run her own business. She very much enjoys working for other people. She recently got her first job as a hostess at the nicest seafood restaurant in our city. The managers were very impressed with her work ethic, ability, and attitude. They call her Rock Star! She enjoys getting a paycheck and she has set up three bank accounts to meet her financial goals: one for checking and two for savings. Her checking account is for regular day-to-day spending. The first savings account is for mid-term future needs, a computer, and a car, etc. The other savings account is for her future living. She has not wavered from her dream of studying in New York City.

NYU is her first choice. She knows it will be a costly venture and she is determined to save as much money as she can now to help realize her near-future dreams.

Real estate investing is not something she shows any interest in, and that is okay. She does show interest in understanding how money works and what she needs to do to be successful in her own path.

My son came to me at age nine. He overheard me talking with Brigitte about my successes and he asked, "Dad, how can I make money?"

I stopped and looked him in the eyes. I wasn't expecting that question from a nine-year-old. I replied, "Well, there is my lawnmower and there is my trimmer. Why don't you walk around our neighborhood and ask who needs their lawn cut?"

My son did just that and picked up five clients that summer. They were very impressed with him and his work ethic and attention to detail. I gladly gave up my free time to invest in my son's growth. I went with him to each client and helped him get more. I helped him create marketing materials and went with him to encourage him to go door-to-door to solicit new clients.

My son has built that business up. He purchased a small riding lawnmower, a trailer that he pulls behind it to haul his push mower, trimmer, and gas. He has been doing his business for five years. He leaves after school and returns home by 8:30 after taking care of his clients' properties. Half of his clients are corporate. My son is thirteen years old and averages between $65 and $75 an hour. That is way more than most adults.

He saves every penny. He has a goal. Since age nine, he has been determined to buy a fourplex for his first property, and he plans to do it by age eighteen. He also wants to ensure that he has at least two bedrooms in his unit so he can have a roommate. His early understanding of real estate investing will serve him well. He is on track to buy his fourplex. I have no doubt that he will have enough cash saved for a down payment.

I encourage any young people to follow this advice. Forget the dream of owning a single-family home. If you want to get ahead financially, sacrifice your desire for that dream home in favor of investing in an income property. Live in it for a year or two and then leverage that property to buy your next. Do it again. Buy another multi-family home. Live in it, leverage it, and then buy again. If you do this for a few years, you will never have to work unless you want to. You will have financial freedom and you will be able to retire early.

Don't rely on a job to get you ahead. Your job is a means to an end. Only you can get yourself ahead. Take calculated risks and don't let fear hold you back, especially if you are starting young. You have room to make mistakes and recover from them financially. Be bold.

This book touched on many aspects of my life and my investment journey. It also glossed over some of my missed opportunities. You can't regret what you did or didn't do in the past, but you can learn from it.

One deal I am glad I walked away from was the commercial building. It was one of the most unique old buildings and I had always admired it. When the opportunity came to buy it, I jumped on it. It was an emotional purchase. I did not look at it the way I did with most of my investments. Ultimately, I realized that I would have been overpaying for the building. The commercial tenants were not necessarily secure (which was not disclosed to me). The tenants in the apartments above were also in really low rents. One was the owners' son and the owners themselves insisted on remaining as tenants. They wanted to dictate the rent they would pay. I soon realized that this was not a good investment. I walked.

There were other missed opportunities, but there is no point in hashing them out. They are in the past where they will remain. Look forward to your future and don't regret the past. Learn from it.

Some other advice that I have is to not enter this world of real estate investment blindly. Do your research. Learn the laws and regulations that govern landlords and tenants. It may seem boring, but read the residential tenancies legislation act in your region and make sure you are doing what is required of a landlord. Don't make decisions based on your heart or gut. Make decisions based on the governing laws, rules, and regulations.

Also, do not rush to rent a unit. It is far cheaper to let a unit sit vacant than to evict a bad tenant. A bad tenant will cost you more than a month or two of vacancies.

Build a kitty for each unit. Have money set aside to deal with repairs, vacancies, and anything that may be unexpected.

Treat tenants with respect. They are your bread and butter. Not all tenants are bad, but when you do experience a bad tenant—and you will—do not paint all tenants with the same brush. Be levelheaded when dealing with tenant concerns. Even if they are not levelheaded, rise above and be the calm that controls the situation. Having said that, don't put up with poor behavior.

Have proper insurance. Don't just decide to turn a property into a short-term rental or student housing without looking into and obtaining the proper insurance coverage. Don't go for the cheapest insurance, go for proper and full coverage. Protect your investment!

Nobody will care about your business as much as you do. Do not offload important aspects such as finding a new tenant. I would be cautious about using a realtor for such an important aspect. Often, realtors do not vet who they put into a rental. They are incentivized by the payout they get for finding a tenant, not for finding a great tenant.

Do not fall for sob stories. In fact, the first sign of a sob story should be the moment you reject an applicant. There is no reason for a sob story. Pity seekers are only trying to manipulate you and will likely end up being problem tenants.

You need to do full background checks on tenants. Use software such as Singlekey.com (I am not paid by them to say this). I have used their services, and if you are a new landlord or even a seasoned landlord who has been burned by a bad tenant, get their rent guarantee. It is worth the peace of mind. Besides, it is a tax write-off.

Do not accept any documentation from your prospective tenant. Documents are so easily forged. I don't trust anything a tenant wants to willingly hand me.

Ask for proof of income. Get a letter from an employer and, where possible, insist it be on company letterhead. Then check the facts. Call the employer, and don't just rely on the number the prospective tenant provided. Google the company number. Ask for the prospective tenant's references by name. Maybe they work for the company, maybe they don't. That is a great way to find a legitimate reference.

Ask good questions of references. When I called a previous landlord for a reference, I asked them to confirm the dates the applicant was a tenant. I also ask them how many properties they owned and what address the prospective tenant lived in. You would be surprised at how many references stumble when you ask how many properties they own and how many get the address wrong. Why, you might ask? Because they are a phoney reference.

Prescreen your applicants. Ask the following questions before you agree to show the unit:

What is your full name?

How many people will be living there?

What are the ages of the people who will be living there?

What is the relationship between the people who will live there?

What is your source(s) of income?

Do you have any pets? If so, what breed?

When are you looking to move in?

Why are you looking to move in?

Get a copy of their driver's license and check it against any existing databases that may verify its authenticity. For example, in Ontario, Canada, where I am from, you can check on the government's website for the authenticity of a license. https://www.dlc.rus.mto.gov.on.ca/dlc/

Google "Driver License Check" in your region.

I have seen many landlords lament after a professional tenant faked all documentation. My question is, was a thorough tenant check performed? Why wasn't the fake documentation recognized in the first place? Protect your investment!

Bad tenants are inevitable. I tell people that it is not if, it is when. At some point, a tenant will screw you over.

The degree to which you will get screwed remains to be seen. Don't lose sleep over it. It will pass, eventually. Weather the storm and do what you can to ride it out. Remember, it is a business. Don't let your emotions overshadow your control and decisions. I have had several bad tenants and have experienced close to the worst through damage and non-payment. Even still, with those negative experiences, I am way ahead financially because I am a real estate investor. I do not regret the past situations. Having said that, I likely could have avoided most, if not all, by holding out for better tenants.

Get a good chartered accountant. Not a bookkeeper or someone you know who is good at filing taxes. Use the proper person with the expertise to help you grow your business. Select a chartered accountant who is familiar with real estate investing. Don't just ask them to do your taxes. Sit down with them. Discuss your goals. Ask for advice on how to structure your portfolio. Does it make sense to register a corporation to shelter your properties from any lawsuits or claims?

Corporations bring a lot of advantages. Often there are tax advantages to having your properties in a corporation. There may be borrowing advantages. Banks often favor corporations and will extend loans easier than to a private individual. When a private individual applies to a bank for a loan or mortgage, the banks may only consider 50 percent of rental income to account for vacancies, etc.

Personally, I have never had 50 percent of my units vacant at the same time. What is interesting though is that the same bank counted 100 percent of a corporation's rental income. How fair is that? Knowing this could make a difference in how you begin your investment portfolio.

If you are already an investor, it isn't as simple as opening a corporation and signing your properties over to the corporation. That could trigger capital gains taxes as if you had sold all your properties.

Bottom line, you should only trust the advice from a chartered accountant.

They say nothing comes easy and there is no fast track to wealth. I guess it depends on what you consider a fast track. If you are disciplined and grow your investment portfolio properly, take care of your properties and screen for the best tenants possible. Only then will you be on a fast(*ish*) track to wealth. It is possible to pull off wealth and success in less than a decade through real estate investing. I consider less than a decade quite quick to becoming wealthy.

I set out to write this book because I did something extraordinary that literally anyone can do. I used debt to create wealth. It goes against the grain of everything we were taught about money and finances, but I am living proof that it works. If you speak to any seasoned real estate investor, they will likely tell you the same thing. Debt = money.

I hope you found this book useful and encouraging as you begin or continue with your own real estate investment journey. Don't listen to the naysayers . . . They don't believe in you.

I believe in you!

Thank you for taking the time to read about my journey.

Good luck with yours!

www.ingramcontent.com/pod-product-compliance
Lightning Source LLC
Chambersburg PA
CBHW071220210326
41597CB00016B/1888